Write
from the
HEART

Lesbians Healing from Heartache

Write
from the
HEART

Lesbians Healing from Heartache

An Anthology

Anita L. Pace, ed.

Questions and answers
by Dakota Sands, MSW

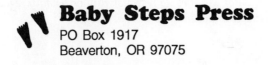

Baby Steps Press
PO Box 1917
Beaverton, OR 97075

Published in the United States by Baby Steps Press, PO Box 1917, Beaverton, Oregon 97075.

First Edition. First Printing.

Cover Design & Artwork: Nancy Vanderburgh, Your Type Typesetting.

Typesetting: Your Type Typesetting, 1509 SE Holly, Portland, Oregon

ISBN 0-9631666-0-3

Library of Congress Catalog Card Number: 91-91474

Printed in the United States.

- ♥ **Write From the Heart–Lesbians Healing from Heartache** has no connection with *Write From the Heart: Writing Workshops for Women,* taught by Lesléa Newman.

- ♥ "Love after love after love after and finally" is reprinted from *Love Me Like You Mean It,* © 1987, Lesléa Newman, HerBooks, Santa Cruz, California.

- ♥ "Red, White and Fucking Blue" is part of a collection of short stories by Lesléa Newman entitled *Every Woman's Dream* (forthcoming).

- ♥ "Attacks of the Heart: Easing the Pain of a Lost Love" was previously printed in *Off Our Backs, A Women's News Journal,* Washington, D.C. and is reprinted with permission.

- ♥ "On Velvet Paw" by Sue McConnell-Celi was previously published in *Network,* a New Jersey monthly lesbian and gay magazine.

The publisher/editor assumes no responsibility or liability regarding the contents of any stories or poems other than her own.

Dedication

This book is dedicated to all the wonderful women who shared their stories and feelings on these pages.

It is also dedicated to my friends Khris, Cindy, David, and Karen, and to my therapists/friends Doris and Shirley who were there for me at varying times when my heart was broken. I also dedicate this book to my Aunt Connie and Uncle John. You all have supported me, defended me, believed in me, and gave me someone to trust. Without you, I don't know how I could have gone on at times.

And to my dad, Gaetano J. Pace, who died during the production of this book, I also dedicate this work. After you died, I found copies of published articles I'd sent you that you kept. Although your words were not always encouraging, you'd also say, "Don't hide your light under a bushel."

I was able to publish this book because of funds left me by my father.

TABLE OF CONTENTS

PART II   Loss Without Choice–When She Dies

EPILOG   One Last Thought

Acknowledgments

I would like to thank all those who helped this book come about.

♥ First of all, thanks to all the women who sent their stories and poems. This book would not exist without you.

♥ Thank you to **Sheila Sofian** for her special editorial assistance.

♥ Thank you to **Janet Lawson** for helping in the development of certain aspects of the contracts with the authors.

♥ Thank you to **Dakota Sands** for your development of the questions and answers throughout the book.

♥ Thank you to **Rev. Vincent Munden** for tremendous support during my last breakup.

♥ Thank you to **Berdell Moffet** for helping me to self-publish this book by her instruction.

♥ Thank you to **Diane Tonkin** for helping me through art therapy.

♥ Thank you to **Susan Gregg** for assisting in the printing of press releases.

♥ Thank you to **Irene Reti** for answering self publishing questions.

♥ Thank you to **Lillene Fifield** for taking the time on short notice to review the book for me.

♥ Thank you to my typesetter, **Nancy Vanderburgh** of Your Type Typesetting for her expertise and hard work.

♥ Thank you to **Mickey Lee** for her photography and help with the back cover photo.

♥ Thank you to **Ed Richter** who helped develop a flyer for the book.

♥ Thank you to **Dr. Stanley Gurman** for emotional support for some seven years.

♥ Thank you to **Harriet Carpenter**, my friend, companion and lover for your support and love.

♥ **Many thanks** to those who helped proofread: Roberta Cohen, Harriet Carpenter

And last, but not least, thanks to all my ex-partners who unintentially motivated me to write this book.

i thought she'd be there forever
i thought
i thought wrong

i thought there'd be no life left for me
i thought
i thought wrong.

Anita L. Pace

Introduction

I was in group therapy (for treatment of depression brought on by a breakup) when I got the idea to create a book for lesbians going through the loss of their relationship. At the time, I was a graduate of the zombie stage, but not by much. I was still staying awake far past Johnny and David (and I can't stand the latter) and awakening early the next day with the sensation that life is lousy.

But somewhere in the midst of emotional chaos, I heard a voice, quite appropriate for someone at a psychiatric clinic as I was. "If you have a lemon, make lemonade," I heard cross through my mind. I've always despised that cliché, but I listened, nonetheless. My degree is in social work, but I'd dabbled in writing for years. The thought that I could produce a book about lesbians healing from breakups seemed possible, if only I weren't so damned depressed.

So one step at a time, I made movements that would lead to an eventual completion. I'd learned about baby steps while completely housebound from massive onslaughts of panic attacks, resulting in agoraphobia.

I sent press releases to more than 30 states as well as to Canada, New Zealand, and Australia. (One story included in this book is, indeed, from New Zealand.) When I received my first story, I tore open the envelope and read it in the post office. I felt as if I'd just received a letter from the love of my life.

I thought stories would jam my post office box, telling of the pain, emptiness, loss of trust, financial burdens, family problems and desperation brought on by their relationship losses...as well as how these feelings and problems were dealt with. But the stories crept in. I don't know if the trickling in of stories had more to do with lesbians who just didn't want to write about the subject or with unpublished press releases. I know there wasn't a scarcity of lesbians who have experienced a relationship loss...or two...or three...or...

But the stories did arrive, usually with a letter to the effect of gratitude that this book was being created. "There is a need for it," many wrote. "Writing this story has been part of my healing process." These letters and the stories gave me the impetus to continue the project when my voice of doubt discouraged me. "You can't get a book published," the voice would say. "Where are you going to get the money?" it asked.

There were blocks of time when I didn't work on the book, especially when I prepared to move from Los Angeles to Portland, but it was always in my head. I'm very grateful to everyone who wrote their stories and sent notes of their gratitude and encouragement. Without them, there'd be no such book still. In fact, in the course of bringing this book together, I spoke by telephone to several of the authors. And several letters were exchanged between myself and some authors on a personal level. That was extremely gratifying for me.

One avenue I took to accumulate more stories was to contact lesbian therapists. I thought they might mention this project to their clients going through a loss.

When I called Dakota Sands, a licensed psychotherapist, she was so enthused with the premise of such an anthology that she wanted to personally participate. Sands' contribution to the book consists of often-asked questions and her answers to them. These are interspersed throughout the book and offer professional opinions in addition to the personal insights of the individual authors.

I decided early into the project that the book would have three purposes: 1) to help lesbians going through a relationship loss by their reading this book; 2) to help those who find comfort and healing by writing their own story; and 3) to help me get over my own loss.

I attempted to have a publisher take on this project, but when several lesbian and/or woman-oriented publishers declined for one reason or another, I decided to self-publish. I did not want to wait two years for the book, once accepted, to be published. And I did not want a publisher possibly eliminating some stories. As a writer who has received many rejection letters and rejection in relationships, I emphasized stories that were written from the heart over stories that were simply well-written. That's why I decided to name this book **Write From the Heart...Lesbians Healing from Heartache**. Nonetheless, most of the stories I received were fine pieces of writing. I reluctantly decided to eliminate two stories and a poem because the authors moved and I couldn't locate them. For legal reasons, I was advised not to print them.

I was pleasantly surprised by the unique ways the authors shared their stories. I'd thought each story would basically say, "She did this and she did that and I was in pain, but I did such and such to help myself." That may have been the theme, but the variations were not duplicated. At this writing, no other book exists for lesbians, by lesbians, about this subject. And none that I know of exists for lesbians whose partner died. Because of that, I encouraged these widows to write their stories. The responses were few, but I am grateful for those who did share about a subject none of us is eager to face. The following is an excerpt from a letter sent me:

"I have never written anything before. I started at the beginning of my story to try and get to the ending. In truth, my story has no ending as yet and at this point with my inner struggles, I don't know if it ever will...I do not yet have a personal private telephone of my own and my phone calls are monitored by an 82 year old snoop who, unfortunately, is my mother. I'm so deep in the closet I am terrified of calls because of the third degree I get. Even worse, she listens on the extension. Hard to believe this is written by a 58 year old woman, divorced 20 years, mother of three grown daughters and grandmother to nine. Enclosed are poems or thoughts I have written to my deceased love. I have a story of a loved woman and her death and how I have been struggling over the past 10 years."

That letter was dated August 29, 1990. At the end of that letter, she wrote, "August 31, 7:30 pm. I told my 19 year old granddaughter I was gay and told her if she didn't want anything more to do with me or would be embarrassed by this knowledge, I would understand. She rushed over and hugged and kissed me and said, 'Grams, I've always loved you. With your trusting me to be the first one to come out to, I love you even more than ever.' Maybe there is a beginning of an ending to my story."

This letter was sent by Doralyn Moran. Besides her poems and story entitled "Life, Death, Reality, Life Again," Lyn has sent several letters expressing her progress, beginning with getting her own phone. Less than a year ago, Lyn was severely depressed and left her home for not much more than going to therapy. On August 1, 1991, she received a Certificate of Completion for Radiation and Safety Techniques and continues toward her goal to become a Registered Dental Nurse.

Doralyn's story of recovering from loss has been an encouragement to me and I imagine to everyone.

A letter from an anonymous author also moved me:

"I...would like to share my story. A month ago, I could not have shared it, but now I feel strong and believe I'm healing myself. The first time I met 'Lisa'...I was to taken by her beauty and her charm. I couldn't believe she would even look my way. But when we were introduced and I looked into her eyes, I felt reassured...We laughed together, cried together, did many things, shared many

thoughts. I only had her such a short six months and I shall always treasure that.

"My loss, at first, was unbearable. I was so alone, so terribly lonely, so pathetic, so sad, completely worthless to everyone. My heart was empty...I cried until I was sick. I lost 43 pounds. I lost sleep...My work meant nothing. My health meant nothing. I really didn't care if I lived or died...

"When does it get better? Everyone says time heals all things. Perhaps. I have to admit, one month ago I still could not talk about her...I tried to imagine she was away on a trip and couldn't write or call. Oh, dear God, how I hated the telephone, looking at it and knowing it wouldn't ring...

"All I know is that I survived. But why? To be alone again? To grow older by myself? To wish for my Lisa to return and know it cannot be?...I think it would be better if I could just die..."

That letter blatantly expresses the grief and hopelessness of loss. And lesbian relationship losses are often, if not always, more painful because of attitudes towards our relationships to begin with. When our relationships aren't taken seriously, neither is our pain if they end. What a tragedy to be aching and have relatives say or think, "Maybe you'll marry a man now."

This project has helped me, even if it didn't stop the pain completely. It didn't stop me thinking about what happened, or get me to stop wondering why it happened. But putting this book together gave me a reason to get up everyday. That's where I think we start when emotional pain has knocked us down. My hope is that this book might help you believe there is light at the end of your tunnel and eventually see it and go through it. For those of you reading this book for purposes other than going through a loss, I hope your inner strength will deepen by your absorption of others' experiences. It may not be so different from what you've known at some time in your life...and something you want never to experience again.

Anita L. Pace
May, 1992

Part I

She Left, I Left,
I Wish I Left Sooner,
I Wish She Left Sooner...

I Wish I Left First

I have searched myself
and found a shell

   brittle, due to the loss of tears

   fragile, due to the loss of one

and so terribly cold.

                    Jessica Fair Stevens

Intimate Betrayal
by Kaye Hunter

I thought I was going to die. My chest hurt, my breath caught in my throat, and a sickening, nauseous feeling swept over me instantly. Death, at that particular moment, would have been a welcomed escape. Dawn's words hit me with all the force of a physical blow.

"I'm having an affair with Amy...I think I love her...I love you, too...What do I do now?"

Tears dammed my eyes, blurring my vision of the scenic park where she had chosen to tell me this secret. My shaking hands could no longer hold my cigarette. This kind of thing happened to other people, not me, not my loyal, compassionate Dawn. I had listened sympathetically while friends told me similar tales of infidelity, all along congratulating myself on my perfect union with a wonderful woman.

From the moment of her confession, I knew I would never again know true happiness. I knew I would never recover from the magnitude of this betrayal. I knew I would never love again. Eight years we had been together. Eight years of my life had been wasted on this woman I suddenly no longer knew. Dawn now loved someone else, and though she claimed to love me also, I felt absolutely alone for the first time in my life. She had tossed me aside, sharing the most intimate part of our life with another woman.

I never knew that one person could cry so many tears, and the pain of my loss was at times more than I thought I could bear. Sleep would not come to my rescue for many nights. Daily tasks became more than I could handle. Simply walking to the mailbox was a labor beyond my strength. I cannot remember how I got through those first few days.

Nothing could shake the constant ache within. I would wake to a new day, dreading everything that lay ahead. Some days it took awhile to remember where the dread came from, but soon I realized my world had ended the day Dawn told me she was sleeping with another woman. Or did it end the first time they kissed? The first time they embraced? The first time they made love? I wondered about these things constantly.

I have known Dawn for as long as I can remember. We never met, we simply grew up together. In high school we became lovers. Groping, silly, inexperienced lovers. Though words like lesbian and gay were foreign to us, we fell hopelessly in love. Innocently, we tossed around terms of endearment, and "I love you's" like they were normal for two teenage best friends. We acknowledged jealousies of boys and other girls, and spent inordinate amounts of time with each other. Together, we planned our lives and eventually left our respective nests.

Somewhere along the way we discovered other women who loved each other. We learned that they were lesbians, proud of their lives and accomplishments. We met several couples and became part of a group of loving, stable women. Coming out was an exciting process and each day was full of new possibilities. Dawn and I had been together longer than most of our friends, and I enjoyed the comfort of our relationship. I loved her more than I thought it possible to love anyone. For awhile everything was perfect.

I graduated from college and began my teaching career. Colleagues became friends and confidants. Soon, I found myself sharing my life openly with straight people without fear of harassment or judgments. I longed to tell my parents about my union with Dawn, but I feared they would blame and hate this girl they had known since childhood.

By the time I decided to come out to people I worked with, Dawn and I had been through all the trials that threaten young romances. The years had strengthened our union, and being out to those around us helped validate our commitment. Now we were as comfortable in the presence of straight couples as we were in the company of gay couples. I was happy until the scaffolding of our carefully-built world began to crumble.

Long and hot, the summer of 1989 seemed endless. Depression had been the overriding theme of those miserable months. Dawn and I never saw one another and I felt us slowly drifting apart. We systematically went through each day fighting in the morning, crying and apologizing by phone in the afternoons, making love at night, only to find ourselves at each other's throats with each new sunrise. My memory bank recalls this time in blurred images and fragmented snatches of heated arguments between the woman I loved most and myself.

We were slowly losing ground. Problems in our lives were reeling out of control. Dawn was unhappy and demanding. Candlelit dinners, designed to bridge the ever-growing distance between us, erupted in screams of anger. Accusations and insults became part of our daily dialogue. Dawn talked incessantly about Amy, a co-worker, and phone bills revealed many calls to her small town, all conveniently made when I was away from our home.

I yearned to go back and feel those secret taboo feelings that we had shared so long ago. I spent money we didn't have on gifts for her, in hopes of somehow regaining that excitement we had shared so long ago. I denied problems, Dawn actively sought solutions. She found her solutions in a woman she fell in love with, before allowing herself to fall out of love with me.

As the school year approached, I became completely absorbed in preparations for my new class. Things as home calmed somewhat, and in the company of other people we looked as if we had never been happier. Beneath the surface, however, our relationship seethed with unresolved problems and conversations we were too afraid to have. My birthday came with the traditional flowers and a sentimental card. Somehow I convinced myself that we had once again survived the rough waters all relationships encounter.

As September ended and we began planning a fall camping trip with several other couples, I sensed I would not be part of that trip. On a bright Indian summer afternoon in early October, Dawn and I found ourselves in a park discussing life's unfair blows. We had just attended a funeral of a friend who died of AIDS. The funeral left us both in pensive moods, pondering the injustices of our world. For some reason, Dawn chose this place and time to tell me about her three month affair with her "friend" Amy. Nothing in my life had prepared me for the complete devastation that lay ahead.

That night, I had to leave. I desperately needed to get away from her and sift through my multi-layers of emotion. I ended up in a smoke-filled bar with two friends, teachers I worked with. Through tears of anguish, I told them my story. While one held my hand, they listened intently to my ramblings.

"How am I supposed to work like this?" I cried.

"You aren't going to work," responded my rational friend, "at least not tomorrow. Call in, take the day off and rest–think through your options. You won't be of any use to your kids like this."

I knew she was right. Teaching is a strenuous job and a teacher cannot afford to face twenty-two energetic children when she is an emotional wreck. Two days later, exhausted and emotionally spent, I returned to work. Just getting through the day until the final bell rang became my goal. I would like to say that as a teacher I was dedicated enough to separate my personal and professional lives, but that was not the case. I hated the demands of my job and was angry that mundane things continued when my life was in such turmoil.

My deepest regret at the time was that I could not turn to my parents for support. I had never before hurt when I could not lean on my parents. Without their understanding I felt so alone. My parents grieved over the loss of someone they loved like a daughter, but they never completely understood the depths of my sorrow. They could not be there for me because I had chose to exclude them from that part of my life.

Dawn and I had entwined our lives so much that I could not fathom a separation. I could not think past the next few minutes, much less prepare for a life alone. I felt as if Dawn and I had invested many years for nothing. I suddenly viewed our life together as a meaningless union, stripped of all worth and integrity. The years we had spent growing into young women were now wasted. Accomplishments that I had once been so proud of vanished under her cloud of deception. Priorities were no longer important, and plans for the future meant little to me. I valued nothing of our past, and hated her for tarnishing my once-treasured memories. Only after realizing that a relationship doesn't have to last forever to be considered worthwhile did I begin to heal. Recovery is a slow and painful process. I fought it much of the time. I somehow felt that by going on with my life, I was telling the world that Dawn had never meant anything to me. Eventually, I acknowledged that moving on with my life was not an admission that I had squandered precious years on a mistake.

Moving from our home was the hardest thing I have ever had to do. It was important that I be the one to move out, because I didn't think I could stand being left twice; once emotionally, once physically. Little remained from our original one bedroom, closet-sized apartment, when we finally split our belonging in that three bedroom brick home. We had come full circle, me back to a one-bedroom apartment and her to a mobile home with her new lover. I could not have made that initial move without the help of some wonderful friends.

I had always considered myself a strong independent woman. Invariably, people were on my sofa telling tales of betrayal and disastrous break-ups. I listened sympathetically, not realizing at the time that I couldn't understand the pain of that kind of loss. Suddenly, I found myself in the homes of friends, talking about facing life alone, hoping for a few words of comfort. My colleagues became my source of strength. I chose them to confide in because they were more my friends than Dawn's. The lesbian couples we ran around with were both our friends, and more than anything, I did not want to put them in the position of having to choose sides. So, during the last weekend of October, while Dawn went camping with our buddies, I moved my things into a small apartment and slowly began putting the pieces of my shattered life back together.

I won't pretend that the rebuilding went smoothly. At times I was fine, then for no apparent reason I would find myself in a heap on the floor, crying and screaming at some invisible force that had ruined my life. Rage would bubble to the surface and erupt, destroying anything and anyone in my path. I was lucky, or maybe even smart, because I surrounded myself with people who could take my abuse and not condemn me when I lost control.

My life changed when I fell in love. I never had a beginning with Dawn, so this new development was enthralling and enticing. Each moment with Lynn was something to anticipate with pleasure. I remember in vivid detail how I felt the first time we kissed. No one in my life had ever been as open as Lynn, and I was terrified in the beginning that something would ruin this new chance at happiness. Soon, however, I learned that Lynn would not allow me to hide my unresolved feelings about Dawn. I wept openly in her arms while she comforted me through my grief. Encouraging me to express my innermost feelings helped in my process of healing.

This period in my life was thwarted with growth. My self-esteem and confidence increased. Once again, my teaching job became important and my sense of pride in who I was became acute. Gone were my insecurities of my past. Gone were the worries of dealing with someone who lacked impulse control. Gone were the days when simply deciding what to wear would cause tremendous grief. Once again I had myself.

Any loss takes time to get over. With the help of a strong network of friends and a newfound inner strength, I survived, even thrived. Learning to be patient with myself and allowing myself to experience all levels of emotions were the keys to my continuance. Ceasing to live was not a choice for me, and learning to live without Dawn has been a challenge, but accepting my new life is constantly rewarding.

In the gay community, when so many of us are estranged from our families, it is imperative that we build strong ties with one another. Our survival as individuals and as families depend on it. We must support each other or our foundations will crack and crumble.

My memories of good times with Dawn are no longer tarnished. They are now pearls that I treasure. I did not waste eight years with the wrong mate. I spent those years wisely, investing in the woman I am now, a woman who is strong, confident, and prepared to endure whatever life hands her.

Juliet

She seems to be on my mind all the time now...
   just as J thought J was getting over her.
The images of the way she smiled
   and eyes twinkled.
Jt was as if she saw into my soul
   knowing my every thought...
Her voice so warm and sweet,
   still filters through my ears,
   down my body...
as a warm flood of emotion melts the darkness.

Romeo

Red, White and Fucking Blue
by Lesléa Newman

You want to know why I'm eating blue spaghetti with tomato sauce and tofu all by myself on the fourth of July? There's a simple, logical, one-word explanation: Margaret.

She left me. I was looking forward to spending a whole day with her smack dab in the middle of the week. You know, we'd get up late, make love, hang out, drink coffee, go back to bed, have a picnic, watch the fireworks. Well, that was the plan, but it seems my Margaret was off somewhere making fireworks of her own. With someone else. And, like a poorly written soap opera, I was the last to know.

So, while the rest of Boston was celebrating the birth of our nation, or protesting it (whatever turns you on) I was alone. All by myself with no picnic ingredients, no party to go to, no one to ooh and ahh with down at the Esplanade when it got dark and they shot those babies up in the air. What a bummer.

I moped around most of the day and then I snapped out of it. I had no right to feel sorry for myself. I was young, healthy, employed, and reasonably good-looking, with a roof over my head and food on the table. That's when I decided, what the heck, I'd make myself a festive meal and have a private celebration. Hell, I'm a woman of the nineties. I don't need anyone else, right? I can take care of myself.

So, due to the day being what it was, and me being the cornball that I am, the meal had to be red, white and blue. I opened the refrigerator and immediately saw red: a jar of Paul Newman's tomato sauce. Perfect. Red was for blood, anger, revenge—how dare that bitch leave me for somebody else? I'm the best thing that ever happened to her. And she knew it, too. Or used to know it.

Now I was feeling blue. Blue food was trickier. I didn't have any blueberries in the fridge. On to the pantry. Would navy beans count? Hardly. How about a can of green beans? Almost, but not quite. Although some people have trouble telling the difference between blue and green and some people don't even think there is a difference. I found that out a few years ago when I was waiting for the T at Harvard Square. A music student from Japan struck up a conversation with me, pointing at my sweater with her flute case. "That's a nice green sweater," she said, though my sweater happened to be blue. When I told her that, she smiled and said there was only one word for blue and green in Japanese, which sounded quite lovely and meant the color of the water. I started wishing that train would never come, but of course it did, and off I went, and three days later I met Margaret, as a matter of fact. But I refuse to think about that right now. Anyway, the point is, if I was Japanese, the green beans would do just fine, but then if I was Japanese, I'm sure I wouldn't give a flying fuck about the fourth of July.

Back to the pantry. That's when I spotted those little bottles full of food coloring–red, green, yellow and blue. I'd gotten them last year for St. Patrick's Day, to make bona fide green mashed potatoes for Margaret. The blue bottle was still full. What could I dye with it?

Why, spaghetti, of course. We used to color spaghetti when I taught day care. We'd save this special activity for a freezing Friday in February when the kids were off the wall from being cooped up all week, and the teachers were bananas from five days of dealing with seventeen pairs of mittens, boots, snow boots, scarves, sweaters, hats and jackets. To while away the afternoon, we'd cook up a huge vat of spaghetti, dye it different colors and throw it against the wall, where it would stick, making a mural I'm sure Picasso himself would have been proud of.

I put up a pot of water, contemplating blue: sadness, an ocean of tears, Lady Day singing the blues, red roses for a blue lady, that was me all right. Sigh.

Two down, one to go. White. Like every good dyke, I didn't have any white bread, white flour, white sugar or white rice in my cupboard, but I did have that handy dandy item no lesbian household is complete without: a virgin block of tofu, sitting on the top shelf of the fridge in a bowl of water. I chopped it up, thinking about white: a blank page, empty space, tabula rasa, clean sheets, starting over, yeah.

So I set the table and sat down with my very own red, white and blue meal, feeling angry, empty and sad. To tell you the truth, the plate in front of me wasn't very appealing. I took a bite anyway, and swallowed. Not too bad, actually. A little chewy maybe, but other than that, okay. After I forced four bites down past the lump in my throat, it hit me: it wasn't just the fourth of July I was celebrating; it was Independence Day. I was celebrating my independence by eating a completely ridiculous meal, and the best part about it was I didn't have to explain it or justify it or defend it or hide it or even share it with anyone. I tell you, the fifth bite was delicious, and after that the food just started tasting better and better. As a matter of fact, I don't ever remember spaghetti tasting so good. I ate it with my fingers, I had seconds and then thirds, I let the sauce drip down my chin, I picked up the plate and licked it clean. Yum yum yum. My country 'tis of me.

I thought I knew my partner, but she changed. Did I only think she loved me? I thought we were so close and that I could trust her. How is it that one so loved and trusted is now a stranger, unworthy of trust, and just plain toxic to me?

This is the most asked question in my private practice. I assure you that your partner's leaving doesn't mean she didn't love you. It may mean she wasn't able to love you the way you needed to be loved or the particular way you wanted. She loved you the best she could with what love capacity she had. You are thinking in black or white terms, which the situation is not. I encourage you as I encourage clients to remember that we all fall short of giving to the degree we might want to.

Progress, not perfection
by Rachel D.

The swimming pool was refreshing under the clear bright afternoon Italian sky. Diane and I had spent the night trying to sleep on the musty train from Milan, arriving hot and exhausted in Florence at 6:00 a.m. We had sat and recuperated in a small sidewalk café, drinking coffee and reading about this new city.

"David's only open this morning," she said, looking up from her brochure of the Academy Gallery where Michaelangelo's masterpiece stood.

I looked at her. After 20 years of living with her, I knew what that look meant. Tired or not, we were heading off to the gallery.

We'd met in college in 1967. Wearing a cotton spring suit covered with little blue flowers, I had sat in the resident associate's dorm room, scared, trying to act like an adult. I was 18 years old. Diane walked in, and the RA introduced us as dorm mates. Her light brown hair, pudgy face, and dark glasses reminded me of a farmer's daughter. Later I discovered that's what she was.

I fell in love with her a year later when I realized she laughed at my jokes. Her infectious smile warmed my budding lesbo heart. Her laughter bolstered my self-esteem and let me imagine the impossible. Winning a gold medal in the Olympics or getting a Nobel Prize would not have equaled the act of kissing her.

One night, I told her. "I think I'm gay."

"I'm straight," she replied, quickly. "What can I do?"

"Oh, I just wanted you to know that." Chicken.

A few months later, I managed to tell her that I loved her. She was happy to hear it. No one had ever loved her before.

Later she said, "I love you, too. I just don't want to lead you on."

"I'm glad to know you love me." I was. I was happy.

That feeling lasted about a day, until I realized it wasn't enough. I wanted to touch her body, hold her, kiss those farmer's lips, so virginal, so pure.

It was a poem that made her defenses melt, one of the many I wrote in my college classes, staring glassy-eyed at the professor while my mind frantically raced through synonyms and aching emotions.

If I reach out to touch you not out of sexual need
But out of love, will you understand?

I know you well and love you
I want to know you better and love you more
My love tells me to touch you, to reach out
And to glide my fingertips across your skin
To know you—for you are a body as well as a mind.

Because I want to love you as a total person...
If I reach out to touch you not out of sexual need
But out of love, will you understand...and respond?

She did. She reached out her hand, and I took it and kissed it. Then I kissed her on the lips.

The cool water in the pool flowed around my tired tourist muscles, relaxing me. I looked at my body in the water, thinking back to David's body that morning. I had stood beneath him, tears of joy streaming down my face. I thought of his long, carved marble right arm hanging at his side, his self-assured stance as he sized up Goliath in the distance. His hands were beautiful. He was perfect. I had never been near such perfection. My life in comparison was in such shambles.

How does one describe so many years? After we graduated from college, we had bought a house in the suburbs. The first day was like any other day in the universe, except the keys to a newly built three bedroom split level house were stuffed in my jeans pocket along with my red Swiss army knife. I stood in the empty kitchen surveying the backyard, wondering who was going to seed the lawn and mow the green expanse. Diane yelled from the living room and I got to the large picture window in time to see a dilapidated maroon pickup truck driving down the street precariously balancing a white Kenmore frost-free refrigerator that was almost as tall as the pickup truck was long.

"Well, he promised us the refrigerator today." We laughed and squeezed hands.

Every summer I mowed the lawn, whenever Diane told me to. As I mowed, I would listen to the opera on my Sony Walkman. She had made me a holder, sewn from a worn-out pair of jeans. It strapped criss-cross around my chest and it kept the radio clean from the flying cuttings. Unfortunately, when I turned my head, painful static would mix with Luciano Pavarotti's rich tenor voice. Once I noticed a little tree frog frantically hopping in front of the deadly blades. I stopped the lawn mower. The scared amphibian stopped as well, his little heart beating as if it would burst. I knelt down and rested with him, ready to give first aid if need be, and then gently directed him toward the edge of the lawn. I only started up the loud cutting machine again when I knew my little friend was safe and sound. I found out later Diane had been watching, laughing, from our bedroom window while she folded the clean-scented wash.

The first couple of years we had the lawn mower tuned up at Sears, but then Diane suggested that I tune it. She got me a book entitled I Hate My Lawn Mower. On the first page, I was reprimanded for buying a lawn mower with an electric starter. Eventually, I got so good at tuning ours that I branched out and went around to the neighborhood husbands asking them if they wanted theirs tuned up as well. The highlight was the year I had five Briggs and Stratton lawn mowers lined up, parts everywhere, my hands covered with smelly oil and black grease. With the flywheel puller, set of torque wrenches, and the Reader's Digest fix-it-yourself book that Diane had bought me, I was in seventh heaven. I never did learn how to repair that electric starter, though.

We had two parties every year. In the summer, we'd have a big barbecue.

"I hear a car door," Diane had said that first year from the kitchen where she was preparing shrimp kabobs and pasta salad.

"It's Patti and George," I'd said, looking out. From the dining room door, I'd called out, "I'll be down in a minute. Pull out a few weeds while you're waiting." The builder had installed a small brick patio in the back, and we'd had to maintain constant vigilance to prevent the green intruders from taking over the red bricks. As I went down with a tray of gin and tonics, I heard voices and wondered who else had arrived. Chatting with Patti and George were the next door neighbor twins Bobby and Billy. Both three year olds, crammed into one patio chair, were being quite sociable and asking for more dip. It was pretty funny.

Eventually, we had built a big 20 x 20 foot wooden deck in the back and parties didn't have quite that same spontaneous haphazardousness. Unless, that is, you don't count the time it rained and I'd cooked out wearing a blue rain slicker, balancing a big umbrella and glass of scotch while waving my hamburger flipper to Patti and George and the other couples. They all waved back at me from the warmth of the dry family room.

The other party was a pre-Christmas international dinner. Every year it was another country. The first year was Brazilian food, because our friends Maria and Enrique had just returned from Brazil. Diane and Maria had cooked it, filling the kitchen with rich aromas, but it wasn't until 10:00 p.m. that we'd finally sat down to the sumptuous meal. After that, we made it an international potluck dinner. The French year I only remember watching Diane make seemingly hundreds of crepes, and the Mexican year I only remember the margaritas. I'd always sit at one end of the long dining room table while Diane was at the other end. Our friends—Patti and George, Maria and Enrique, Bill and Sharon, Peter and Sue—all sat around the sides of the table. The room lit up with friendly banter about winter snow storms, kids' accomplishments, good food, and remember-when stories. Every year I felt the same pit in my stomach, although I never understood it.

Christmas. Diane loved Christmas, and she went all out for it. The house would fill up with the smell of spicy fruitcakes and savory butter cookies. We'd pick up the tree, and I'd carry it in the back of my car to the house. For half a year afterwards, I'd vacuum prickly brown needles out of the crevices of my hatchback. While we'd decorate the tree, Diane would play Christmas carol tapes and we'd get further and further entangled in the strings of Christmas lights.

I'd pull out the tinsel. "No, there's an order to decorating the tree," Diane would remind me, pointing to the other box.

"I know, I know. 'First the lights, then the ornaments, then the tinsel'," I mimicked. Each year, we repeated the dialogue we had had the first year. It made us both laugh. Out came the Christmas ornaments: the silvery blue cloth balls, the creamy white ones, the bright green ones. Then the little mirrors went up, reflecting all the lights.

I'd pull out a small gray box, stuffed with special Christmas orna-ments that we'd collected on our yearly vacation trips around the country. As we'd listen to pa-rum-pa-pum-pum, we'd hang up the swinging glass angel with red wings, the little plastic clowns, the wooden cats and my miniature collection of wrenches and hammers that we'd found one year at a New Hampshire crafts fair. Then Diane and I would sit close together on the couch, looking at our masterpiece, taking in the fresh evergreen smell, and toasting ourselves and Christ-mas with glasses of rum-spiked eggnog. All this from a Jewish person.

On our second to last vacation together, we went to North Carolina, camping with Patti and George. I'd come back with an exact balsa wood model of the glider flown by the Wright brothers at Kitty Hawk. I'd spent that spring sitting on the deck putting it together. As a kid, I'd always gotten comfort putting model planes together. It cleared my head, I guess. I knew I was drinking too much. Diane and I were each getting so deeply engrossed in our respective careers that we barely spoke the same language anymore. I was feeling less and less comfort-able hidden away in heterosexual suburbia, pretending I belonged. Diane liked it the way it was.

The beginning of the end was my affair with a lesbian-identified woman in 1985. Karen and I would make passionate addictive love every chance we got. For the first time ever, I had begun lying to Diane. Instead of slaving on my dissertation at school, I would spend evenings pouring popcorn over Karen's lithe body, slowly undoing her lace panties, pushing kernels of popcorn into her deep wet crotch, fishing them out with my tongue. Fueled by wine and pent-up lesbian fantasies, I would ignore the pain of the situation for a few hours in wild unin-hibited lust.

My therapist had said I had the inner strength to do whatever I wanted with my life. I could continue being taken care of by Diane in a homophobic, straight-identified, closeted world, or be free and open in a lesbian community with a lesbian-identified partner. I cried on the rare occasions that we made love. I cried when I masturbated. I knew something was wrong, yet the thought of leaving her terrified me.

"I know what she's thinking," I'd said. Diane and I were sitting in my therapist's office.

"No you don't," said my therapist.

"After all these years with her, yes I do."

"You two are totally enmeshed." She held her short hands clasped together. "I can separate you." Her hands pulled apart to become two equals, together but not enmeshed. I stared at her hands. They were close, but not touching.

Afterwards, Diane and I had sat and drank coffee. "What do you think?" I had asked.

"There's no point in going to couples therapy," she had said. "I'm not going to change. I'm straight. I like the way I am."

"And I like the way I am." Flashes of Karen's agile body above me, her hands slowly tracing down my stomach, her voice mesmerizing, and my body exploding into a hot crashing orgasm. "I like the way I am," I'd repeated.

We looked at each other. It was over.

Diane was motioning that it was time to get ready for dinner. I turned over in the lazy water and got out of the pool. On the return from our European vacation, we would divide up 20 years of collected possessions, and I would pack my stuff and leave. Maybe because it was an Italian villa, maybe because we had seen David that day, or maybe just because we knew it would be the very last time, we made love that evening before going to dinner. I hid my tears from her.

The last day was like any other day in the universe except I got up at 6:00 a.m. and hugged Diane good-bye. We stood at the bottom of the stairs and hugged like two little trained monkeys wrapping their arms around each other, performing for a circus audience, as if we were supposed to be doing this. I reached into my pocket and fished out my house keys and gave them to her. I felt my Swiss army knife safe in my pocket, along with the receipt for the things I had had shipped. Then I got into my car, packed with a set of torque wrenches, a flywheel puller, a model of the Wright brothers Kitty Hawk glider, and a small, half-filled gray box of Christmas ornaments. I headed west, alone, to California.

I got angry at her a year later when she moved in with another woman. We wrote hurtful letters to each other until I told her to stop contacting me while I faced my anger. I took eight months to get a perspective, during which time I stopped drinking and joined both Alcoholics Anonymous and Al-Anon. I realized it was all about me, that her choices for her life had nothing to do with me. If I left her because she told me she was 'straight' and it took me 18 years to hear her, it was my choice. Her getting involved with another woman would be her choice. It didn't make her a different person, nor invalidate all the years we'd had together nor the love we still share.

That first year I marched in the Los Angeles Gay Pride Parade with the gay scientists. Barely able to remember the names of my new acquaintances, my ears burned the entire afternoon, not from the hot sun, but from the fear of being so visible. At the end of the day, we rested on the grass in front of a West Hollywood women's bar, checking out the sights. Gay men and lesbians were milling around, walking hand in hand with their lovers. In cars just returning to Santa Monica Boulevard, heterosexual couples looked straight ahead. I was very mellow, reveling in how free I felt.

"I can't believe how we took over the streets for a whole day," I commented to friends.

"Hey, it's all in your attitude."

Two years after I left Diane, I went to a cemetery and buried my need for her. I sat on the cold dank ground and cried, listening to a Spanish song about reaching to the sky for beautiful dreams. The singer said she had found her dreams in the strong trees she planted on Earth for herself. I stared at the photo album filled with years and years of us, always together, like two little pea pods growing together in the same garden. Was I ever alone in all those years? Who was I? I stared at my own face for a long time. Just who was more homophobic? I took off the ring she had given me in 1969 and put it in a tiny purple box, never to be looked at again.

At a family gathering, I made a "coming out" speech. Although most family members knew about my lifestyle, I had never talked about it, and, of course, neither had they. "If one is gay and homophobic," I said, "it is self-hate; a self-hatred sustained by society's lack of validation for one's self and of one's choice of a mate. I've been working on overcoming my own homophobia. So has my mother, who has been trying to fix me up with someone. Don't worry–she's a nice Jewish doctor."

Everyone laughed. I felt my ears turning red, but I laughed too. "Coming out is a process," I continued. "We're never fully out and we should never stop trying to keep coming out, whatever we have to come out from under: from homophobia, from fear of not being loved, or from fear of being alone. When we come out, when we shed our self-hatred and accept ourselves for who we are, we become free. 'Coming out has to be better for the soul than passing through life in various shades of invisibility.'" (*Twice Blessed: On Being Lesbian, Gay and Jewish*, Christie Balka and Andy Rose (eds.), Boston: Beacon Press, 1989, p. 56)

My aunt came up to me and hugged me later. No one else did. I realized it didn't matter. I was coming out to myself, not to them.

Three years after I left Diane, I marched again, wearing a bright T-shirt that announced I am a gay scientist. "Hey, way to go!!" Friends called to me from the immense throng of excited spectators.

"I'm jealous," Steve said, marching next to me. "You must jump in and out of every bar in town."

I smiled, then ran off to hug someone else. These were my lesbian AA and Al-Anon friends calling to me, supporting me, loving me.

I walked through the gay festival with Mimi and Cindy and Fran and Sue, looking at the jewelry, pushing our way through the crowd of thousands.

"What do you think?" I held up a 14K gold earring showing linked women's symbols.

"It's great. Looks better than the Lambda," Cindy said.

"Yeah. Some people might not know what Lambda means. I want 'em to know."

The day came when I woke up one morning and asked my 'inner child' what she wanted for breakfast. She said, "Pancakes! I want those French pancakes!" I dragged out the crepe maker and made them for her, laughing and singing with her while she sat at the kitchen counter with those big wide eyes and silly crooked glasses, telling me about her dreams and her coloring book. She wants to be Michaelangelo when she grows up. Standing in the sweet-smelling kitchen, I realized that cooking and cleaning were a joy since I was doing these things for her. I worried a little that the pancakes weren't perfect, but I stopped myself. I felt happy and realized that the promises of AA were coming true. I was comprehending the word "serenity" and knowing peace. I was taking care of myself and keeping the focus where it belonged. On me. I love that little girl.

That night, I called Diane because we hadn't talked in a while.

"I made pancakes for myself this morning," I told her.

"You cooked for yourself?"

"I know, it's hard to believe. They were good, too."

"That's real progress," she said.

"Yeah, progress, not perfection. Perfection is for Italian marble sculptures, not for people."

She laughed.

So did I.

The Love

Rememberance of time
and place,

up keep and daily maintenance.

Dates, appointments to keep.

Night of plenty
contained

treasured
untainted.

In the understood relations,

for the triangle of ours

I wrote.

Of love, lust, and our loss...

Jessica Fair Stevens

Walking Through Fire
by Cris Newport

It took me a year before I could look at the photograph of a dinner that was to celebrate my graduation from UMass; a year before I could stare down the table to the end where my ex-lover sat next to the woman she left me for. When I first got the pictures back, I didn't even open them. The fact that I can look at them now is a reflection of not only how far I've come, but also how far I still have to go.

I have always believed that each experience in my life happens for a reason: the time, the place, the people who touch my life and whose lives I touch. All these various elements come together to create the vibrant tapestry I alone can weave for myself. I have needed this faith to bring me back into the world from my inner sabbatical. For the first time ever, when I lost X, I grieved, deeply and for a long time.

We don't talk enough to each other about grieving. We don't allow ourselves to feel bad, to admit we're depressed and anxious. We hide the deep circles under our eyes, attribute our rapid weight loss to "stress." Perhaps we're afraid our friends won't understand, or that they'll get bored with our stories. Or that they'll want us just to "get over it." But unless we commit to the journey, we never get over it.

My experience with X and the journey I've made over the past year and a half to come to this place is not uncommon. The external situation is familiar to every lesbian who's ever taken the chance and loved another woman, to any woman who's ever taken the chance and loved. The plot is simple: I am involved in a long term monogamous relationship. But something is missing. I love my lover, but I feel hollow and unfulfilled. Then I meet someone. Someone who is so unlike myself, someone who opens a place inside me I never knew existed. I leave my lover for this new relationship. My new lover leaves someone to be with me. We are blissfully happy. Briefly. Then we hear the places where the music is strained, the discord. We begin to see we are different people. We have "issues." We have fights. She becomes attracted to someone else. She tells me it's nothing. I want to believe her. She sleeps with this new woman. I am devastated. We break up.

The story is reflected in our literature, in each offering from the lesbian presses reaffirming that we can find new people, that we can find love again, that we can discard our old lives and our old lovers and figure we'll work it out later. Passion calls us, and we respond to that call. But the literature does not explore our deepest moments of self-doubt, of darkness, of fear and anxiety as we wait for the phone to ring and to be told we are no longer desirable. We are no longer part of a couple. We are alone again. How do we survive these partings after so much has passed between us? I never thought about it much before last year. Now, I think about it all the time. We live in a throw-away culture. We consume the goods and discard the packaging. When X slept with someone else, I felt as though I'd been thrown away, and it took me a long time to believe that I was worthy of love again.

X and I met at a point in my life when I'd finally started to come out of my head and into my body. I was struggling with this movement in my fiction, primarily, working toward expressing what my characters were feeling, not just what they thought. X blew into my life like a whirlwind. I found myself attracted to her but had no intention of acting on it. I was involved. I'd felt this way before and had gotten over it with time. But on the day she handed me a note, I knew what it said even before I'd opened it. I knew this time would be different.

I barely hesitated before saying yes to this feeling. I had never even considered taking such a risk. My life was built upon rigid structures, learned as a child to fend off the chaos of an abusive home. I was afraid to take chances and had, up to that point, been willing to settle for companionship with my lover. But I found myself yearning for the kind of openness I saw in X. She ran into the wind. She seduced me with her words and attitudes before she ever touched my body. I was mesmerized by this attitude. How could this freedom be possible? Could I be like this? I was a child hanging upside down from a tree. Everything looked different. And I liked the new perspective.

So I jumped in. For almost eight weeks, I sailed like a free-falling sky diver. I had never felt so alive before. Every morning, I would feel excitement course through me when I woke up. It was late fall, and the world was spinning down toward winter. The colors that are so vibrant in the Northeastern autumns were all but gone. But everything seemed so alive. I remember standing in the glass-encased catwalk of the university. It was just sunset. On my left, the sky was smeared with colors–red and orange at the horizon, melding into green, then indigo, then midnight blue. On my right, the full moon was rising. I was suspended in time between night and day. That twilight place was, as it is in faerie stories, the place where magic abounds. Every moment was like that. And I believed it was because of X. Her love, her passion, focused on me, made me feel as though I was the center of the universe. I could be anything.

Beyond the window of her bedroom, there was a line of fir trees. I used to lie awake after we made love, and, while she slept, I would watch Orion rise above the tree line and travel in his nightly journey across the sky. He was my protector, my hunter, and I was Orion–protector, hunter–spinning through the sky over the dark bedroom, night after night.

By the time reality set in and we began to recognize and "process" our "issues," I was so deeply in love that I believed I would do anything to hold on to this relationship. I was totally committed to it and believed X when she talked about traveling to Europe after graduation, about raising children together, about moving in together in the fall, about making a permanent commitment to each other. This is what I have been moving toward all my life, I thought. I pushed down my fear when she withdrew. I began to mould myself into someone I didn't recognize. It's change, I told myself. I'm changing. I need this chaos to break down the structures. I will be free when I've moved through this place...

And while I was free and moving through the chaos, X was no longer with me. I have regretted, at times, the fact that I said yes to her in the first place. I have hated myself for letting myself believe her lies. I have been ashamed and embarrassed. I have wept in the night and held a bottle of sleeping pills in my hands believing I was not strong enough to continue, that death would be a more comforting embrace then my own two arms and my own solidarity with myself could ever be. I remember sitting in the bathroom at three a.m. thinking, "I am not strong enough for this," and for the first time feeling no obstacle in my path. When I realized that the choice of life or death was truly mine, that I was ultimately not responsible to anyone else, I was able to get up, put the pills away and go back to bed. I didn't sleep much that night. I had struck bottom. I could begin my journey back.

X demanded an openness I could not match. I was battered from a series of bad relationships and from the violence in my family. Somewhere inside me there was a child locked away who craved the openness, the freedom. But the adult did not want to be exposed. We fought about freedom and space more than anything else, and the fact that X wanted to be able to tell her friends all about our relationship, from what we did in bed to the issues I brought with me from the past. I was so frightened. I wanted to trust her, but I couldn't. I was afraid to set limits, to say no. I was afraid if I said no, she would leave me and I would shrivel up and die; curl back in on myself again and never feel the wind on my face or see the colors of the sunrise. When I finally did say no, she was furious with me. She felt contained by my need for safety. She acted as if my needs were a cage. I backed down.

When it became clear that something was stirring with a mutual acquaintance, Susan, I was unable to set limits. Instead, I responded to X from a place of panic and fear instead of from a place of strength. She assured me there was nothing there. They were "just friends." I tried to believe her, even though all the gossip reports from our too-close circle of friends said otherwise.

By this time it was late spring, early summer. Our shared dreams were starting to unravel. We no longer talked of raising children (we had discussed names), of marriage, of traveling Europe together. We talked about Susan. I began to feel as though my life was no longer in my control. I was coming apart. I couldn't eat or sleep. I don't remember the job I had, nor the people I worked with. I threw up every morning and waited by the phone every evening for X to call. I needed constant reassurance. And while I could step back and see how my behavior was beginning to tear the relationship apart, I could not stop myself. I tried to control X. She fought me.

In September, it was clear that we had reached a crisis point. One afternoon we met downtown. It was a beautiful day, and we walked the streets together. I had thought we'd spend the evening together, but she had other plans. We sat on a park bench. I watched the soccer players and envied them their joy. I was crying and shaking. Finally I said, "You've already decided, haven't you?"

"Yes."

I asked her to call me that night. She hesitated, gave in. I waited until the last train had arrived in the suburb where she lived before I called the house. No answer. I knew where she was, and I cried.

The next day I bounced between rage and despair. I begged her not to let our relationship end. She said it didn't have to. I was relieved. I tried to convince myself that I could "do" non-monogamy, that this attraction would blow itself apart in a matter of months. I could hang on that long. After all, I was a new person. A risk taker. But, really, I had become a person I didn't even know. I had no more demands to make. I was silenced, invisible. Just as I had always been. It was familiar.

But somewhere, deep inside, I had doubts. After two weeks, I called her on the phone and told her I couldn't do it. It was terribly important to me at the time that I be the first to say those words. I was tired of being left, even though I already had been.

In the months that followed, I spent a lot of time with Anne, the woman who X had left for me. The more we talked, the more the strange behavior I found in X made sense. When some of my things were returned from Susan, I found a love letter X had written to Susan during our vacation, during a time she professed she was thinking of no one but me. Now I knew it as a lie and I began to understand how she had lied to me for a long, long time. Although she couldn't accept or work within the limits that felt safe for me, she'd told me she could and reassured me, but sent me into a downward spiral. In the fall I began a demanding program at graduate school and had little time to consider these other matters. It gave me the psychic space I needed to begin to heal.

What did I do to heal myself? Even now, as I look back the answers are not clear. There was no one thing, no magic formula. But there were many ways in which I cared for myself during that time as I grieved for the loss of someone I had trusted and loved. I talked to my friends daily on the telephone. I asked for help. I didn't need advice and I got none, but I did get a chance to talk about how I felt and release the pain into the larger world. I also wrote. I wrote hundreds of wrathful letters to X that I never sent. I poured out my rage and disappointment. I always felt better afterward. I worked. I read books, but this was harder as my mind did tend to drift.

I began working intensively with the Tarot. I used the cards to get in touch with how I was feeling. I meditated. I cried. I allowed myself to feel sad and angry and hurt. I didn't sensor my feelings or pass judgment on them. I just let it happen. This, I think, was the most important thing I could have done.

In January I went to a well-known psychic for a reading. We talked for a long about the healing process I had embarked on and then I asked her about X. She affirmed my own observations. X was "seductive" in her energy, but it was "all show and no go." I had to laugh. It was so true. It was as though once the chase was won and you were a powerless captive, the fun went out of it. I had thought that more than once and had berated myself for being a willing captive. Now, I understood that I had been bewitched, in a sense, and was spellbound until I'd looked to the power within to free me.

This psychic also affirmed my choice of silence between X and myself, said we were speaking different languages. X's anger, which had been such an intrinsic part of our relationship, was a furious, childlike statement of self. I could feel the pain behind the anger, but I could also see the vicious circle it trapped X in. I had always been able to feel her pain and confusion and had tried to help, to fix things. But that was a role for which I was not suited. None of us are. We can only bear witness and hold the one who cries in our arms. We can only offer comfort to the other for her pain; we cannot take it away. I had believed that X ran toward what was easier. When things between us became hard, she turned her passion and energy toward Susan. I felt the wind shift, and that was what had sent me into a panic. This deflection of pain on X's part was so much a part of who she was when we were together. It was never her fault. She was always blameless. I had blamed myself. Now I knew it was not my fault.

I listened to the tape of that reading again recently. I say the chant to myself about letting her go in light and love. I say the chant to myself that if we are to have contact with each other at some point in the future, may it be because it is right for both of us. I struggle to let her go.

Time is a funny thing. It is late spring again, and I find that I miss her. And while I reread my journals to remind myself that she is not the person with whom I can be myself, and I am not the person with whom she can be happy, I still miss her. I don't want her back. I like the person I have become in this past year, and I like who I am becoming. I have walked through the fire. The silence between us still feels right. I will be leaving this city soon and will be glad to have a new physical and psychic space in which to continue to grow.

I have lost many of my friends who returned to the university with X and Susan last fall. We cannot seem to find ways to talk around the fact of X's existence, and I am not comfortable knowing too much about her present life. It's easier for me when I cannot imagine her living in a particular part of town, or seeing certain people, or walking down the street with one or another of my friends. What saddens me most about this experience is that the friends I made at the university were women with whom I took enormous risks. These were the first women I trusted without sleeping with. I loved each of them in a special way and mourn the loss of their company as deeply as I mourned the loss of X.

But I do not regret the chance I took. I am living in my body every day now. I am finding joy again in my life. I have reached out to a new lover with whom I am able to be simply myself. We are both in the throes of transformation and sometimes our sadness overwhelms the time we spend together. But I am learning about what loving detachment means. I am learning that I can hold her and dry her tears, but I do not have to fix things. I am her partner, not her parent, or sibling, or therapist. I am simply who I am. She loves me for that. I love myself for that as well. I am whole, and she shares my wholeness. We are not looking to complete or fix each other, but to join. And every night, when I lie down beside her, I am thankful that I didn't take my life that night, because now I really have something to live for: Me.

I feel empty, as if there's a hole in my gut. I crave the physical affection from my ex. I can't sleep well, I'm restless, and I wake up in pain. What can I do?

 What you're facing are the effects of losing someone who has meant the world to you. Loss of any magnitude brings about change and with change there is resistance, for change can mean uncertainty. Now is the time to surround yourself with people you can feel safe and comfortable with. Find an object that will comfort you through the night like a bathrobe that you can wear and snuggle up to. Or use a pillow, yours, not hers. Change the room around. Re-arrange the furniture. The empty feelings will lessen and disappear after awhile. This is what the first stage of grieving feels like.

The Trusting Game

The trusting game
a frustrating game to play
and J trusted you
believed every word you'd say

The tears are pourin' down
from my eyes
just like the rain
J don't understand the meaning
of the word anymore
and "trusting"
is a difficult word to ignore

J don't understand
what this golden ring was for
Oh this golden ring
Was it worth the sting?

But the challenge of the game
is to trust again
and J'll use what J've learned
from the lessons of getting burned

The trusting game
a frustrating game to play
and J trusted you
Js there anything more to say?

Words and Music by
Marie Skonieczny, ©1991

attacks of the heart:
easing the pain of a lost love
by zana

Oh joy! the how-to article you've been waiting for! be sure to save this in a special place for the next time the need arises.

i want you to know i'm writing this fresh on the spot, after two and a half months of sheer hell. you do, in time, get some perspective back, maybe even a sense of humor. and it can be sooner rather than later if you just regard the whole thing as an illness that can be helped by time-honored remedies. here are a few that have worked for me:

1) don't pretend nothing's wrong. a whole lot is wrong. you feel abandoned, unloved, maybe even betrayed, and just generally like it's the end of the world. you'll never find another lover like this one, right? so wallow in it, at least when you're all alone. cry a lot. write voluminous journal entries. feel real sorry for yourself.

2) get away from HER. don't feel you have to be "nice," friendly, or politically correct. if it's hard to be around her, don't. if you happen to be living on the same land, working at the same job, and/or have all the same friends, you have my deepest empathy. do the best you can. and give yourself a lot of credit–it's not easy. take any sort of vacations you can manage, even just a weekend at someone else's house.

3) be with friends–but not too much. it's good and reassuring to hang out with old friends. let them see that you're obsessed and miserable–it shows a mile away anyhow. so you go to a movie with them and everybody has a good time but you, because some actress reminded

you of HER. it's okay. it's all perfectly natural. your friends will lose interest in being with you after you've pooped enough parties. that's okay, too–it won't last forever. don't spend *all* your time trying to socialize, anyway; you'll just end up feeling lousy because they're so normal and you're not. let's face it, you have so little to give right now and are a drain on other people's energy. so–

4) be alone–but not too much. get into some interesting projects, or just do nice mindless work like cleaning everything in the house. that will leave you plenty of time to ponder endlessly what went wrong, how it could have been avoided, and what you'll do differently if there is a next time. these thoughts won't hurt you. when they start getting tedious, do something that *does* require your thinking processes. or go be with friends and let them distract you.

5) meet new people–but not too much. remember, you're not at your best. if others find you a drag, spaced-out, preoccupied with her, they're not going to be too hot for your friendship. then you'll feel even more worthless and unlovable. so go slow. don't attach yourself to a new person. get to know her a little at a time. try to listen to who she is–and not *just* as a potential new lover.

6) SHE is not replaceable. true, you can have another lover sometime, but you can't just replace HER like a defective carburetor. don't try to fill up that hole in your heart too soon. learn a few things from it all first. get to know yourself again–who *are* you these days, anyway? and what about all those feelings of connectedness you used to have with this beautiful earth–take some time to reaffirm and strengthen those. let *life* be your only lover for awhile. the next special woman will come along in all good time.

7) be a lover to yourself. give yourself flowers, or candy, or a new wrench–whatever's your favorite indulgence. stay in bed late, call in sick and go to the park, take long baths, make love with yourself, cook special dishes just for you. wear your nicest clothes. smile at that lovely woman in the mirror!

8) consult any articles like this one that you've stashed away for a rainy day, or maybe *motherwit*, the tarot, *womanspirit*, *the kwan yin book of changes*, whatever might give comfort or insight. i have a little red book in which i copy my favorite wise sayings; when i need counsel i open it at random and always find something i can use. maybe

somebody else's gems of wisdom won't seem right for you. but they'll give you something to bounce off of, to find what *is* right.

9) new, new, new—nu? sure, there were wonderful things about HER that you don't want to forget. but right now, take a break. collect all those thises and thats lurking around your place and pack them away for awhile. put some other stuff on your altar, on the walls—maybe a drawing done by another friend, or a special stone you find in the woods. maybe you want to start an herb garden or make some new curtains. change your environment to remind yourself that you're changing. your life's not over, and it doesn't have to be stuck back there in the past. start in on your future!

after a dream

it feels like i am being
punched in the stomach
i have loved a woman for nine
years and the tide is
going out on our relationship
and there is nothing
i can do to stop it so
i wake up not knowing
where i am
(i am in cleveland)
and i wake up feeling
empty inside and there is
no one and i wake up and
it is just me with
this empty bed.

Susan J. Friedman

The woman I was with decided she wasn't a Lesbian and says she can't be in the relationship any longer. At the same time, she says she loves me. I'm confused and devastated. How could this have happened?

 Unfortunately and dreadful as it may be, drastic changes are the reality of breakups when we involve ourselves with partners who aren't Lesbian-identified. Being woman-identified is part of our claim to "Lesbianhood." The other part reaches deeper and that is more difficult to define because our Lesbian identity is unique for each of us. The common thread is a feeling of being "home" in the love and loving to make love with a woman. I advise avoiding women (for lover relationships) who aren't Lesbian-identified.

My Sweet Little Kid
by Janet Lawson

This isn't a story about a loss. It's about finding someone. I want to introduce you to Janet, my little kid. I think she is about three years old. Feel her soft brown hair and look at those big round hazel eyes. Isn't she cute? She is very sensitive and caring. And boy is she smart! I call her "Little Janet." Why just yesterday she had me laughing at some very witty stuff she said. I'm real glad I found her.

She's been lost so long. Well, "lost" isn't exactly the right word. She's been there all along but I didn't know it. She was afraid to come out directly, so she's been just sneaking a peek at the world now and then. I didn't even know she was there until just recently. Our mother was one of those who "did the best they could with what they had." You know what that means. I had picked another lover who was "emotionally unavailable." Oh, it's no big deal, I do it all the time. Except this one was an exact emotional match of our mother. Little Janet freaked out. That's how I found her.

She was pretty traumatized. She kept sobbing. I didn't know how to get her to stop. In desperation, I called Frankie and asked her to come over. Frankie had been gone about a month at the time. She said she'd left because she "needed her space." I left a message on her answering machine. Little Janet cried and cried. We both begged Frankie to come over, but she wouldn't. Frankie said I had to parent my own little kid. I didn't know what the hell that meant. I still wasn't too sure who Little Janet was and she sure as hell didn't want to come out and expose herself. But her pain that came out that night filled up every square inch of my being. That was the first time I came face to face with her, and I didn't know what to do with it. I wasn't even sure what "it" was, but it hurt like hell.

Frankie steadfastly refused to come over that night when we finally got her on the telephone. She had spilled jelly or something all over the front seat of her car and said she had to clean it up. Little Janet and I cried ourselves to sleep.

After that, I fought hard to stay in control. Everyone knows people get together and break up all the time. It's a fact of life. After you break up, it hurts for awhile and then you get over it. You become friends. It's the lesbian thing to do. You each find another lover. In time, you find yourself at parties and gatherings with your ex-lovers and your new lover and their new lovers. If you live in a small community it can get rather complicated eventually, so you learn to get along. Everyone is civilized and, most importantly, you never talk about the pain. Because it is over. After all, you each have another lover now and so what's the point? I worked at keeping it together. I knew that was expected of me, and that being angry, resentful, and a "whining weanie" was not acceptable. I was supposed to get over it, and by God I would.

Two weeks before Christmas, I saw Frankie in her truck with another brown-haired girl. Frankie liked brunettes. Young ones. Both of them were smiling. Frankie was grinning from ear to ear. She pulled up next to me at the light and rolled down her window. Her smile got bigger. "How ya doing?" she yelled at me. "Fine," I yelled back, playing the game. The brown-haired girl's face went to a scowl when she looked at me. Then I knew. This was Frankie's new lover. I was going to have to be friends with this woman who couldn't even smile at me. Frankie and I had only been separated about six weeks then. I smiled back at them and waved as the light changed. I knew how to act.

Little Janet ventured out again and asked me not to do it, but I did it anyway. OK, so I had read all of the books by this time, and I knew I was supposed to parent my little kid, but I didn't know how. I hadn't even learned how to listen to her yet. I called Frankie. I got the answering machine again.

"Listen," I told the tape. "I know that girl I saw you with is your new friend. It's Christmastime. I know I have to get over it. Let's be friends."

I knew this was a reasonable thing to do. I'd been moved by the holiday spirit. A Christmas parade and its music had been inspirational. I just knew that "peace and goodwill toward all" was filling every living person's soul, including Frankie's. Little Janet was furious.

"She isn't going to call you back," she screamed at me. "She doesn't care about us, and even if she did, she wouldn't know what to do about it."

Well, this outburst shocked me. Being angry at others was definitely not allowed or acceptable. Being angry was worse than whining. Reasonable people don't do it. There is just no point.

"No," I assured Little Janet patiently, ignoring her anger, "she does care about us. She had a rotten childhood too, and we can't be mean to her just because she can't be there for us. We have to be understanding about these things. After all, it's Christmas. We have to learn to forgive and forget. Get the spirit, OK?"

"But what about me?" wailed Little Janet. Tears welled up in her eyes.

I was exasperated and frustrated. I didn't know how to deal with that little voice. It was becoming very unnerving because I wasn't used to this voice at all, and I didn't have an answer for her. It wasn't the fact that I was talking to myself that concerned me. I've had millions of conversations with myself. In fact, I think I talk to myself more than I talk to anyone else. I have a full committee up there trying to run the show. They keep me going endlessly with the you "shoulds" and the "why-didn't-you" and the "well-so-and-so-really-didn't-mean-it." I just didn't know what to do for this little voice. She was so new she didn't even have a name yet. So I did the best I could. I fixed her a big bowl of her favorite pasta and put her to bed with the teddy bear I got after my first meeting of Adult Children of Alcoholics. I felt more than a little foolish about the bear, but I figured maybe I should start taking some directions from others.

Frankie didn't call, but she did come by and leave a cheery note while we were out. Our house is a boat, so it's easy just to pop in and leave a note. We never lock the boat. I was so glad she had come and left a note. I just knew everything would be okay and that we would be friends, and life would somehow return to normal. Little Janet wasn't quite so sure, and her ever increasing whining "what about me?" was beginning to make me edgy.

"Quit your goddamn whining! You're gonna blow our chance to be friends again with Frankie. If you would just leave it alone this pain would go away for everyone, me and Frankie both. Believe me, I've been through this a thousand times before. You just have to let it go, then the pain will go away. We'll all be friends and it will be over. And once it's over I can get another lover and it will be better next time. I promise, so stop it."

"You always promise," she sniffled. "Nobody cares about me, not even you."

"Jeezus Christ! I do too take care of you! We have a great place to live, I buy you every toy that comes along even when I can't afford it, and I make damn sure there are enough people around for you to play with. Will somebody tell me what the fuck I'm supposed to do to take better care of you?"

"Now you sound just like mom. I'm leaving and I'm never coming back here." Her lower lip trembled.

I didn't see her for almost a week. It was a welcome reprieve. I saw more of Frankie. Her new friend wasn't around. I don't know why. I didn't ask. I didn't even ask her name. Okay, Frankie didn't talk about her either. Not talking about something like that is always your best bet.

Frankie seemed a little depressed, so Little Janet did come out eventually to buy Frankie's little kid a Christmas present. (I told you she was a sweet kid.) We got Frankie a pair of slippers that looked like Miniature Schnauzers. We both knew Frankie wanted them. Little Janet was a lot of fun after that for a whole week. Turns out we both love shopping for others. Each gift has to be just perfect.

Two days before Christmas, Frankie was crying because her mother had told her all she wanted for Christmas was a phone call from her son. I spent the day with her, and I really felt sorry for her. I knew she was in a lot of pain. I wished I could fix it for her. I felt closer to her that day than I had in over two years. I bought her a teddy bear. She held it and cried quiety as we picked out a gift for her mother. We spent the entire day together and didn't fight about anything.

The big day was Christmas Eve. I spent it with Frankie, my nephew, and some friends. We took the boat across the harbor for a nice dinner in a fancy restaurant. Little Janet and I were very excited. We had already given Frankie two beautiful expensive color photographs from a local artist that morning. I knew I had done the right thing by giving them to her, even though I had promised myself I wouldn't, because she had been so depressed because of what her mother said. She looked so happy that it made me feel good.

We have Frankie the Schnauzer slippers. Her little kid squealed with delight when she opened them. She showed them off to everyone, clearly pleased. She later said she knew I would get them for her because being thoughtful was one of my known traits.

Frankie then gave Little Janet and me a bag with a number of small packages in it. We tore into them. There was a pair of sox, a box of crayons, some bubble bath, and a few other small items. As we opened them, Frankie said she didn't have time to get our "main gift" and that we could have it later.

"Thanks, these are cool," was about all I could manage. Little Janet took off without a word. She didn't have to say anything. The rest of the committee supplied a ceaseless monologue throughout the balance of the entire evening.

"Isn't that great? You don't even own a bathtub to sit in. And even if you found a tub to use it in, you're allergic to that stuff. And she knows that. Everyone up here except you knows she doesn't care about us. You're so dumb."

I was numb. I was so numb I didn't do anything when Frankie yelled at me about the sorry condition of my dock lines and how someday someone would get hurt because of them. I stood silently on the bridge as she determined where to tie up the boat in the restaurant berth. I didn't say anything when she chastised me for scooping my nephew's leftover shrimp into a styrofoam cup. I silently eased the forty-one foot yacht out of the slip into a gusty wind with only about twenty feet of clearance while she yelled at me from the lower deck. I smiled at my other friends who congratulated me for getting the boat out safely. I did not create a scene, nor did I say anything to Frankie. I do know how to behave. Finally, everyone went home except my nephew. He's twelve. He was very excited because he was going to Arizona with me in the morning. His Christmas was still ahead of him; the boat was filled with packages bearing his name. I was glad he was there. It kept me from crying myself to sleep again.

We came back from Arizona on the 27th. I called Frankie. Little Janet didn't want anything to do with it. Frankie said it was late and that we could come over in the morning. Little Janet announced she wasn't going. I went over in the morning by myself and she had two presents, a book and a video, that we wanted.

"See," I told Little Janet later, "these are nice and she just ran out of time before Christmas."

Little Janet did not respond. I'm not even sure she was around. The rest of the committee, however, got into the act and once they started up, my life became miserable.

"You don't listen and that's the problem. She went and visited friends in Los Angeles and that's why she didn't get our presents on time. She said so herself. I heard her."

"Look, she was really stressed out about her mother..." I tried to be reasonable with them.

"Yeah, make excuses for her..."

"Stop it, do you hear me? She is just doing the best she can with what she's got..."

How long this tirade went on I cannot say. It seemed like a month at least. Finally, I gave in. I was going to have to confront Frankie on this business of Christmas. It looked as if that was going to be the only way to quiet the committee. I had forgotten about Little Janet completely by this time. All I wanted to do was quiet my mind. Now they were calling me "coward" in addition to the usual stuff.

"Yeah, we know who you are," they taunted me. "Good old peace-at-any-price." Ms. Fix It herself.

They had all read those God-damned self help books with me, and now they had a whole new vocabulary of insulting things to throw at me. I couldn't take it anymore. I made the call. The conversation deteriorated into an argument and in the end she yelled at me.

"Mistakes happen."

That was it. That's all she said. No "I'm sorry I hurt your feelings." No acceptance of any responsibility whatsoever. Just, "mistakes happen." And I accepted that. A truce of sorts was declared. We would once again be pleasant towards each other if there was an occasional accidental meeting.

Time passed. There were no phone calls, no "how are you doing today?" or "how about lunch?" or anything. Little Janet came back. She mostly sat around hurting all the time. She just felt like an open wound, and I still didn't know what to do with her. She didn't say much. She was just looking around all the time, noting all the little painful things in life, like the fact that Frankie had taken down all of the pictures of me in her office and replaced them with pictures of Mary, her new "friend," whose name we now knew. She was also there when we did go to lunch with Frankie and Frankie told us how "healthy" her new relationship was.

In February, Frankie showed up at my office unannounced. She wanted to do the civilized thing and let me know beforehand that she and Mary were going on the Great Outdoors ski trip on the weekend that just happened to fall on my birthday. That's the trip I go on every year. She wanted to assure me personally that they would be very respectful of my feelings and not be openly affectionate in front of me. I felt as if I had been shot. I looked her right in the eye and said,

"I have been in pain every day since the day you left. Some days are better than others, but I hurt every single day."

I don't know where those words came from. That kind of honesty certainly wasn't something I was used to engaging in. Then I added,

"I'll make it easier on everyone. I won't go on the trip."

To her credit, she choked back a few tears as I excused myself to see a client. (I am an attorney.) I got applause from the committee for my response on that one.

"Good for you! You didn't just 'make nice' for once."

"Way to go."

"We're gonna make a woman outta you yet!"

My victory was short-lived, however, because I immediately lapsed into a fullblown case of self-pity for a week. It was terrible. Finally, I decided that I'd go on the trip because I had made plans with friends to go and I had told my nephew he could come also. I didn't want to be a victim anymore. No matter how much it hurt, Goddamn it, I was going. I would face the music and get over it.

The committee liked that decision, too. They can be so fickle.

It was a very strained weekend. I tried like hell to be civilized. Mary wouldn't even look at me, much less talk to me, but Frankie was as cheerful as ever. She even gave me a birthday card upon which she had written, "You deserve the best." Nothing wrong with this picture.

Little Janet hated it. She was miserable. Even the rest of the committee which had taken to congratulating me on my boldness in going in the first place couldn't make her feel better.

"So what?" she cried. "You still haven't figured out who's going to take care of me."

"You got to go skiing. Wasn't that fun?" I asked.

"That's not what I need."

"Look, as soon as I lose thirty pounds, I'll get us another girlfriend. It will be okay then."

This made a few committee members laugh.

"You're never going to lose that thirty pounds. You have been trying for over a year. Get real. Accept the fact that you're fat and forget it."

"Fuck you guys!" I yelled at them. They can be really vicious. That's how the yelling started. And it got worse. Much worse. By April I was constantly furious. I worked myself up into a slow boil, mad at everyone. It was scary. I was beyond mad. Oh, sure, I'd had outbursts of anger before, but in the past I had usually been able to get the lid back on it in a relatively short period of time. This was different. I had thirty eight years of unvented anger festering in me. I was mad at my father for going to prison when I was a baby. I was mad at my grandmother who never calls me. I was mad at my aunts who never visisted me. I was mad at my mother who didn't speak to me for three years because she was mad at me for sticking up for myself. I was mad at my step-father who molested me. I was mad at my sister because she didn't respect my feelings. I was mad at everyone in my life who had failed to be there for me. And I was mad at Frankie for abandoning us.

Once she had told me that I was "relationship material," that she wanted to spend her whole life with me, that I was her "soul mate." She even lied to me when she left me. She said she needed her "space" and that maybe we could get back together again in a year or so. She sounded so sincere when she said it. But instead she got another girlfriend in just six weeks, and then she moved in with her and apparently felt it isn't even necessary to give me her new phone number or address. I felt totally deceived.

By happenstance, I spoke to her about a month ago. She said she "had been thinking" about calling me. It made me furious. All of these weeks and months that I have been alone and the best she can do is tell me she "had been thinking" of calling me. I was livid. I silently ranted and raved and screamed at her for being such a miserable uncaring son-of-a-bitch.

Then it happened. In the middle of another angry screaming session while driving my car, I found Little Janet again. She was sitting in the back seat. Her eyes were huge. Big tears filled them and spilled down her cheeks slowly, one at a time.

"Who is going to take care of me?" she sobbed, choking on her words.

Suddenly my whole being was filled with compassion for this little kid who was never simply loved just because. This little kid always had to please people and take care of them to be noticed. This little kid was never number one for anybody. And suddenly, I knew what I had to do for her. I had to hold her. I had to wipe her tears and tell her she was cute, that she was smart and lovable and that she wasn't too fat to be loved. I told her she didn't have to worry anymore because I wouldn't let her play with Frankie anymore. Or anyone like Frankie.

"How are you gonna do that?" She looked up at me skeptically.

I laughed. "Like this," I said. "Frankie! You can't play with Little Janet anymore until you learn how to treat her nice! How's that?" I smiled.

Little Janet giggled and wiggled up into the front seat.

"You would really do that for me?"

"I think I need to learn to do that for both of us," I said, pulling her into my lap and cuddling her. "Let me work on it and I'll come up with something," I promised her. "I think we need some directions, some rules or guidelines to keep us out of relationships where you get lost. You let me think about it and I'll come up with an answer."

It took a few days, but I did it. I came up with a few simple rules to live by.

- ♥ What lovers say and what they do have to match.

- ♥ They have to be able to take responsibility for their own behavior. If they mess up, they have to be able to say they are sorry.

- ♥ They have to be nice to us.

- ♥ They have to assume an equal share of the responsibility for maintaining the relationship.

My job is to make sure that I see what's really there instead of seeking only what I want to see in them.

So when I figured it all out, I took Little Janet on my knee and I explained it to her. I also told her she could come out more often and that I would try real hard to listen to her when she was afraid or scared. I told her that we would both work together to pick the next lover, someone who would be kind to both of us and who would let us be kind to her back. That seemed to make Little Janet very happy. We said a prayer for Frankie's little kid and slept like babies that night.

In Memory Of

Remember when we used to sigh?
We sit and wonder as we look across the table
into each other's eyes
"I still love you,"
you say to me
Very civilly I respond the same
It is the truth..
But we have lost something
that something that could make us sigh.
You say we've been together a long time...
this was bound to happen
But how could we lose so much?
I felt my place would always be in our bed
my legs spread as I offered myself to you.
I still hear your loving voice
pushing me deeper
taking me beyond my inhibitions.
You weren't afraid of my womanhood...
you reveled in it
Quite a lover you were.

I'm mourning a death
a death of passion
passion that seemed never ending.
Billie Holliday croons in the background
singing of her blues.
Did passion skip out of her life, too?

Every once in awhile
I see passion
Yet, she skips away the moment I glimpse her.
I want to grab her
possess her
make love to her
like I once did you.

I scream at you.
Did you drive passion away?
Did you neglect her in some way?
...did she feel unwanted?

Passion has many faces
I see her fleetingly in
paintings
in things I read
music I hear.
She can be found all around
teasing me
teasing us.
We have long waited for her return
yet
she is not coming back.
She left as fast as she came.
We just didn't know it.

Michelle Bancroft

Jn the Moss Season
by Sara Edelstein

The tree was old, its branches spreading wide, its trunk thick and knobby. On one side of the trunk, a thick covering of moss grew almost to the ground and up to the lower branches. Today the moss was a rich kelly green, and there were pale orange shoots coming from it.

I walked by the mossy tree, as usual, on my way home from work. It had been raining lately, the blustery rains which made a bridge between late winter and early spring, but this afternoon there was a break in the clouds, an elongated triangle of clear sky bordered by a line of cloud. The sky-light shone on the moss, brightening it, heightening the color.

I let the moss hold my attention for a moment, then continued walking home. It was a Friday afternoon. I'd been used to spending Friday night, almost always Friday night and part of the rest of the weekend with Erica. We'd usually have dinner together, sometimes go out, but more often just stay home together that first night of the weekend.

I missed holding Erica...running my fingers through the crisp curliness of her hair...stroking the softness and warmth of her skin, the strong curve of her back.

I missed other things too, like Erica's funny grin as she talked about the day's events at work and all the "crazies" she'd seen. I missed the sudden vulnerability of her face sometimes, and the way her joking could turn serious as she told me some private piece of her life.

They were warming, these thoughts. I could wind them around me like a blanket, burrow down into them as I'd snuggled up against Erica.

I could snap my mind shut around them and almost forget. Almost but not quite. There was still an ache between my breasts which went on and on, a hollowed-out feeling inside me which remembering couldn't fill.

You could have made plans for tonight, I told myself. But I hadn't wanted to do that. It was paradoxical. I was lonely now–lonely again–but I needed time alone. Time to be quiet and let myself remember, or forget, or just let things settle inside me.

I turned the corner of the last short block. Peter, the little boy who lived in the house next to my apartment building, was playing on the front porch, riding back and forth on his tricycle. He shouted "hi" to me, and I waved at him and shouted "hi" back, but I didn't stop to talk to him as I sometimes did.

I climbed the flight of stairs to my apartment. Inside, I hung up my coat, filled the tea kettle, and set it on the stove to boil. When the tea was made, Earl Grey, a taste Erica and I had shared, I sat down with it at the kitchen table.

I'd always liked this corner of my apartment. The pale yellow walls opened into big windows through which I could see the spread of tree branches, winter-bare now, and the second story of the tall white house across the street. The windows faced west, and a brief patch of afternoon sun shone on my plants. I'd had the aluminum plant for a few years. I'd bought the cactus in a bristly mood one day. And the blue ceramic pot which housed a spider plant was a gift Erica had given me for my birthday last August.

I'd thought of giving it away. Or mailing it to Seattle and letting it arrive dead and broken on Erica's doorstep. But I still remembered Erica's warm smile as she handed me her present. And the plant had done so well hanging near my kitchen window that I hadn't the heart to move it.

I inhaled the fragrance of the tea as I poured myself a fresh cup. Plans, I thought. Would I make a plan for the evening, or just let it drift along? Did it matter anyway? I pawed through the spread-out newspaper for the television section. I could watch the news and maybe a M*A*S*H* rerun. Sitting in front of the television might be just what I needed. At eight o'clock, there was an hour program on the wild lions of Africa. I might watch that.

Rice with tofu and vegetables was easy to fix for dinner, and after awhile I started semi-automatically to make it. I'd taken pleasure in cooking dinner for Erica and me on Friday nights when Erica came to my place and we didn't go out to a restaurant. I'd been learning to cook some Thai dishes, spicy soups and curries, which we both enjoyed. But these days I didn't have the energy or the interest to fix anything special. At least I'd progressed from the frozen dinners I'd had every evening for awhile after Erica had ended things between us.

From outside I could hear muted sounds of rush-hour traffic: the hum of a motor, the sibilance of tires moving against pavement, and the faraway blare of a car horn.

It was quiet inside the apartment. The downstairs neighbors, who sometimes played their stereo louder than I liked, were probably out tonight. The quietness stayed with me while I ate dinner at the kitchen table, not in front of the television after all. Let the world be for tonight, I thought. I didn't want to hear about any more earthquakes or bombings or starving children.

Halfway through dinner, the telephone rang. It was Margaret, a friend Erica and I shared, but my friend first. Margaret's voice was warm. "How you doing?" she asked, "Where've you been keeping yourself?"

I laughed a little. "Oh, here and there."

"How about going to a movie tomorrow night with Diane and I? The new Australian one is supposed to be pretty good. Liz and Jane are going, too, so maybe we can all go out for a drink afterward."

I thought for a moment. "Sure. Sounds like fun."

"Come over at six-thirty or so and we'll go together," Margaret suggested.

"Okay," I agreed. "See you then."

A warm feeling stayed inside me after I hung up the phone. Margaret was a good friend. It was cheering to think of spending tomorrow evening with her and the others. Two couples and me alone, of course. That rubbed a nerve. But it couldn't be helped, so I'd just have to get used to it.

I made myself a cup of decaffeinated coffee laced with brandy, my favorite evening drink these days. Ten after seven, the clock said, still almost an hour until the program on lions.

The brandy relaxed me, and I leaned back against the cushions on the couch. I was glad the week was over. Nice as the children in my first grade class were, it would be good not to see them again until Monday.

Perhaps I would read for awhile. My eyes moved along the rows of books on the bookshelf, tracing different sizes and colors. They came to rest on my guitar, sitting on the floor next to the bookcase, the music stand beside it, where I'd left them both a few months ago.

I didn't know if I could play tonight, if I had any music inside me. But maybe if I did play a little, the ache inside would ease. The guitar case was dusty from sitting untouched for so long. Dusty enough to write Erica's name on it. And perhaps I should have. Or mail the dust to her. I grimaced, picturing Erica's uncomprehending look when she opened an envelope filled only with dust.

I took the guitar from its case. The strings cut into my fingers. The calluses were gone from my fingertips, and my hands felt clumsy. But I struggled through a *Bouree* by J.S. Bach and then a Renaissance *Galliard*.

The muscles in my left hand beginning to cramp, I played a piece that Erica had liked: a Peruvian song about a woman of the streets abandoned by her lover. The melody was mournful but beautiful, and although I didn't understand all of the words, I felt a tightness in my chest as I sang along with the chords.

I wouldn't sing that again for Erica, even though Erica spoke of being friends. At our Sunday morning brunch together, the weekend before Erica moved to Seattle, Erica talked about how we could see each other sometimes. I remembered crumpling the cloth napkin in my hands, trying not to cry.

Erica might have been glad to be on her own in Seattle, but I felt emptiness: a hard outer crust, a kind of deadness, and a cold, hurting loneliness inside.

I put away the guitar and made myself another cup of coffee with brandy. It was just about eight o'clock. I might as well watch the program on lions.

Another world filled the screen; tall grasses and lakes and green, verdant hills. I saw land baked dry by the sun in one season and battered by monsoons in another.

In the dry season there were waterholes where the animals came to drink: herds of antelope, startling at an unexpected sound, and small, scurrying rodents. And there a lioness, impassive behind a blind of grasses, stalked her prey.

The lioness was hungry, I could feel that. Hunger ached inside her while she waited. And there was anger, too, still sheathed along with her dangerous claws.

Hours passed and still the lioness watched, while the light changed from bright midday to wheat-colored afternoon. At last the lioness sprang, in one steel-muscled motion, at the straggler in a herd of antelope. Her movement and scent picked up instantly. The rest of the herd bolted, but the lioness had her prey.

The camera moved away then, but I understood what happened next. There beside the waterhole, the lioness satisfied her hunger. Her stomach empty no longer, her teeth and claws ripped through the still-warm flesh, the silky, now bloody skin of the antelope.

The camera moved on to a rose-colored African sunset. On a bare branch, hawk like birds perched, silhouetted against the sunset. They called to each other, and called again, as the sun went down.

A flutesong wound itself around the calls of the birds and the program ended. I got up to turn off the set. It was only nine o'clock, but I was tired. Changing into my pajamas, I made some hot milk with honey and drank it sitting up in bed. Gratefully, tomorrow was Saturday and there was no need to set the alarm.

Turning off the light, I settled myself in bed, pulling the blankets into a warm cocoon. The dark was comforting.

I woke to pale morning light. From my bedroom window I saw rain-dark streets and sidewalks. A light rain was falling and the sky was covered with layers of blue-gray clouds.

The chalky light filled the room. I wasn't sleepy anymore, but I pulled the blankets closer, fighting the sadness that was lying in wait for me. It was there in the bare place on the wall where I'd taken down the picture Erica had given me, and there in the unused pillow next to mine.

I saw, for an instant, Erica's head on the pillow beside me. Erica's arm around me. I could let my mind go further: Erica's face against my breast, Erica's hand tracing the curve of my hips and stomach, the softness of Erica's lips moving along my skin.

I could go on. On and on. But there was no one to journey with me. No one to lie pressed against me as if a single fire ran between us.

Erica was gone. I'd been left; abandoned, alone.

Tearless, my eyes stung. A dull pain, like an indrawn breath held too long, ran down my breastbone and curled itself into a knot in the pit of my stomach.

I closed my eyes and turned on my side, pressing my cheek against the softness of the pillow. Erica, I thought, but there was no voice to answer my call. Except for scraps of paper fluttering towards me. And there were letters, like the one I'd sent to Erica and her reply. In another, I asked Erica not to end things; to think of how much we'd shared and could still be together.

And there was Erica's letter, friendly but cool: we needed a clean break, she needed to be alone on her own in Seattle. She didn't feel as I did and it wasn't any use her pretending otherwise. It was better to be honest, so we could still be friends, and I should come up and visit her in Seattle when I had a chance.

That was almost three months ago. I hadn't written or called Erica in all that time, but I'd gotten a postcard from her once. There was the Space Needle on the front and a few lines on the back; the new job in graphic design was working out well. And her cats liked the new apartment overlooking Puget Sound.

I would have moved up to Seattle with her, subbing for a while if necessary until I could find another teaching job. After over a year together, I'd hoped we could live with each other.

But Erica hadn't wanted that. That had been clear. I wondered why. How could Erica have given so much and then shut off suddenly? True, Erica could suddenly become distant. I'd seen that before. But now it seemed as if there was a part of Erica which I hadn't known. Perhaps a cold steel gate lay beneath her warm surface; a gate which shut tightly when anyone approached too near.

I was the one who talked about living together. After all the years alone, I wanted that. Was that it, then? Was that what made Erica draw so far away?

I could wait outside that gate of Erica's. I could wait aching with hunger, as the lioness had waited. Like the lioness, I could attack with teeth and claws, hurling myself against the gate and wasting my strength on its unyielding surface.

The gate would remain closed. I could see that there was no key. Maybe for someone else Erica would open the gate and smile that tender, warming smile. At least for awhile. But not for me. We could see each other, as Erica said, but it would go no further than that. For me, Erica would never let there be a key.

I opened my eyes. The clock read seven-forty. Outside a dog barked and then someone shouted at the dog. I sat up in bed, wincing as the cold air hit my shoulders.

In the shower, I turned the dial until the water was as hot as I could stand. The water streamed across my back, flowed over my breasts. Touching me, warming me, if only for a moment.

Afterwards, I pulled on old, comfortable clothes: pants, a soft cotton turtleneck shirt, and a sweater. Then there was breakfast, with a cup of coffee while I read part of the newspaper.

After breakfast, I took a walk. It wasn't raining hard now, but a fine mist came down, the droplets soft and warm against my face. I walked along quiet side streets, following without thinking a route I alone, and sometimes Erica and I, had gone along many times. The light rain had stopped completely, but the park was still deserted. The west grass, sponge-like, squashed beneath my feet as I walked across a flat playing field and then up a low hill.

From the top, I could see the roofs of neighboring houses, and beyond them the gently sloping hills which ran along the west side of the city. Those hills were patterned, I knew, with streets and houses and families. But from here all that was invisible. There were only the hills, blue-gray and furred with fog, and the gray-white clouds layered above them.

I drew in a breath and released it slowly. Behind me the grassy hill blended into gray-paved schoolyard. There were basketball hoops, games of hopscotch painted in yellow lines on the cement, and a pole for tether ball.

There would be children playing here soon, breaking into the quiet, laughing and shouting at their games like the energetic six-year-olds in my class at school.

I smiled at the thought as I walked across the field again, stopping for a moment beside a fenced-in community garden where Erica and I had talked about getting a garden plot. There were plots of earth grassed over now, dried corn stalks, and a few bedraggled cabbage and parsley plants growing through the winter.

I might be able to get a space in the garden. Even by myself, it might be nice to plant one. I walked on again, striding along quickly, enjoying the feeling of my muscles working, of warmth flowing through me. At last I circled back towards my apartment.

A few blocks from home, I stopped once again at the moss-covered tree. The moss was lusher still this morning, a flowering of darker and lighter green with edges of golden brown. Here and there tiny raindrops, jewel-like in their clarity, were suspended on the moss.

I reached out my hand and touched the moss. It was faintly moist and as I expected, a velvety softness. I stroked gently with my fingertips and then laid my whole hand against the moss.

With my hand, and with all of me, I felt the aliveness of the moss. There was a gladness to it, a joyful flourishing in the soft, warm rain.

I stood there for a long moment, not wanting to move away. The moss, and the strong old tree it grew upon, were opening to spring. And I would too, I suddenly thought. Even as I walked the last few blocks to my apartment, I still felt the sense of a greenness inside me.

I've been terribly depressed since my lover and I broke up, but my family is just so happy about it. They aren't dancing around, but I can tell by their lack of compassion. It hurts when they make comments about "getting into a normal relationship" now. It hurts that they don't understand my pain and I need their support. If I'd keep away from them, it would just be another loss. What should I do?

Now is not the time to look for your family's support. You need to surround yourself with people who accept you, your choices, and your lesbianism. It's important to immerse yourself in activities, particularly physical ones such as sports, aerobics, and dance. It's time to stay busy with your normal routine. Go to work, care for yourself. You mainly need a support network in the Lesbian/Gay community that accepts you. Staying away from your family doesn't necessarily mean it will be permanent. This is temporary. Until you heal your hurt from the breakup, however, you need to have limited contact with your family. Perhaps phone calls and an occasional visit will be the most you can do and be comfortable with. They will not be able to understand your hurt, as you've described them, and will make you feel lonelier and worse about yourself, instead of seeing yourself for the loving person you are.

Diversity

Running together,   (as you)
in my mind—

the vanguard.

Forerunner of frenzy.

And who am I to write?

Need the writer
be a tortured soul?

Jessica Fair Stevens

Just for a Few Laughs, Darling
by Diane De Moon

There's nothing I can say about the pain except maybe that it only hurts now and then. Okay, I'll try harder. It only hurts when I laugh? It only hurts when I think about the seven wasted years? It only hurts when I think about my bankruptcy? It only hurts when I reminisce about our court date (even though I won)? It only hurts when I think about my nervous breakdown? It only hurts when I think about leaving everything 2000 miles behind to bond with my "no-doubt-about-it -forever lover"? Yeah, it only hurts when I think about her every now and then.

Forgiveness is a challenge. But it's easy to forgive an alcoholic, insane witch. Anger helps too. It's fun to see my "x" for who she really was. I will share a recurring nightmare based on her last words: Her silhouette circles around the full moon. Her costume is complete with a black hat and cape. Her only prop is her broom. And she chants "It was all just for a few laughs, darling." Then she looks into my eyes exposing all three of her teeth. I turn to her and ask "Ha, ha?" The nightmare is less frequent than before, but every now and then it happens–usually when I think about getting involved with someone new. It does serve as a great reminder of things that could be. Talk about flags! I definitely take my time and assess each situation.

People (especially lesbians) get stranger and stranger with time. So does their sense of humor. I wonder why? It's even worse when they become your lover and the joke is on you. Trust becomes nonexistent. The lesbian world is nothing more than the straight world–full of shit! It makes me wonder if "lesbian" was redefined somewhere. If it was and I am not a lesbian anymore, then who am I? If it hasn't been redefined, then who are these impostors? Or did I end up in lesbian hell? Who cares? No one.

All right. Enough is enough. It's all metaphysical, right? What goes around comes around. And there is a happy ending after all. Really there is...positively.

About two years ago, I was faced with the biggest challenge of my life. I had to rebuild emotionally, financially, physically, creatively, spiritually and (God forbid) romantically. It was this or suicide.

I took inventory of my life and wrote about ten goals, tailored by me, for me. I began a journal. When I felt like writing, I did. I kept reminding myself of the goals and I measured my progress. I'd fail. I'd succeed. It was a very dark, sad and lonely time. But as time passed, I began to attain some of the goals and then I'd make new ones. As I wrote in my journal, I realized that there was only one goal to strive for: Happiness. My happiness. I can't imagine anyone not striving for that goal. Then again, there was a time when I didn't.

When I was going through the brunt of the breakup, I was anxiety-stricken and could barely complete a sentence, let alone read. It seemed no one cared or understood. My problem might have seemed quite small in comparison to murder, rape, and other such things, but it must have been a pretty serious problem for me to contemplate suicide. But I felt I had to pull myself out of my own hole. Suicide is too easy and I knew in the back of my mind that my "x" wasn't worth it. Now that's in the forefront of my mind.

I'd moved 2000 miles away from my life to be with my lover. So there I was in a new city, suddenly single, and with the realization that my relationship had been so absorbing that I had no friends. I had no support system. So I had to create one.

I saw two therapists for varying times. They were very helpful guides. And I met countless others along the way whom I am extremely grateful for.

I became aware of negative people around me and I got them out of my life. I only had room for positive people. How'd I know the difference? By how I felt. If I didn't feel good around them, they were gone. My "x" was the first to go. I'd noticed how negativity had a ripple effect that brought about even more negatives. When I started to weed out the negatives and bring in more positives, the ripple effect worked again, but this time the positives became visible and I felt better.

Positive people became guides, showing me the way out of the black hole I'd gotten trapped in. Striving for happiness has helped me attain other goals, all which satellite around the happiness goal. This philosophy has changed my life and made it very satisfying. I am more independent, less lonely, and more motivated to do what I've always wanted. I'm deriving tremendous satisfaction from pursuing a career in music.

My life has begun again with renewed vigor. I've discovered new things, and most importantly, I've discovered what was always there, but ignored previously, because of my preoccupation with my "x."

I never gave up or gave in. I maintained my career through it all. I made some good friends that I think will be long-lasting.

I still think about my "x" every now and then. I forgive her, but I'll never forget her. And I'll never ever become her.

My life isn't over at 36. I can dream again. No more witches. No more nightmares. I am very happy. And I know I'll be happier.

Break-Up, I

J see you in the kitchen
up to the elbows in dirty laundry
you are trying to order the chaos
(and J am afraid if J get too close
to you,
J'll break open...)

J hear you in what was once
your bedroom
watching T.V. and watching more T.V.
J answer you with a word,
not a sentence, a sentence
not a paragraph
(and J'm afraid if J get too close
to you
J'll break open...)

J don't need to read the papers
to see what is going on in Jraq,
Kuwait—
There is chemical warfare in our livingroom—
There is devastation in your face
(and J'm afraid if J get too close
to you
J'll break open...)

Susan J. Friedman

Break-Up, II

One false move and I will be holding her—
One false move and I will be sobbing—
One false move and I will be trying to hold back the tide
with my bare hands
and I will die trying.

Guilt pounds me like a fist
it has the power to beat me as it has so many
times before
The force
of our silence is louder than our loudest
most passionate fight
It is the silence after a death.

Susan J. Friedman

Always and Forever ... Not
by Lupe Anne Reuben

By the time I met Alba, I'd had enough relationships, enough heartaches, and enough therapy to know how to recognize a good relationship and how to create one. But I threw a lot of what I knew straight out the window.

Alba was in her twenties. I'd sworn I'd never get involved with someone in that age group again. Not to say all such women aren't ready for a committed relationship, just the ones I've gotten involved with.

Alba lived with her parents. No way was I going to get involved with such a person, but I thought how Alba had lived on her own for awhile. And because of all her college work, she certainly had no choice but to live at home...I figured.

And I was never going to get involved with a woman who came from a screwed up family. But when I saw that Alba's father was an alcoholic and her mother was a recluse, having no friends and not liking anyone in the house except her family, I thought how everyone comes from a screwed up family. I sure did.

And I let myself believe what I knew wasn't true; not arguing was not necessarily a good sign. But I compared it to my previous relationship of constant bickering and embarrassing scenes in front of others. I closed my eyes and welcomed the apparent peace.

Alba and I spoke for hours on the phone everyday. Actually, I spoke, she listened. Sometimes I thought she just liked hearing another voice.

We spent a lot of time together. We went to lots of movies and out to eat. Alba loved going out to eat. I was used to saving what money I had and cooking a meal here and there, but when Alba wanted to eat out, so did I.

She said she had only one friend, a guy. They'd been involved for several years when she realized she was gay. It broke his heart and she hated hurting him. He wanted her to keep the $2000 engagement ring he'd given her. She did.

Alba had a dry sense of humor and her eyes twinkled when she smiled at me, for awhile, that is. And she seemed very loyal. One day we were outside an auditorium when I introduced her to some people I knew. One woman said to Alba, "You're very attractive." Alba scooted to my side and said, "I'm with her." She was pretty timid. Either way, I sure felt good that she wanted to be with me. I was grateful my last lover left.

We were both shy about being physical, too. When she told me she had been having "p" and "s" feelings toward me, I felt an electrical bolt go through me. Saying "physical" and "sexual" were just too frightening to utter. But that didn't last long. One evening, we were sitting on my sofa. I could feel we were going to exchange a hug or more. The tension was thick and delightfully so. My body hadn't felt that alive in years. I tried wrestling with her to break the sexual block. Nope. We were stiff. We scooted closer to each other. Stiff again. Finally, I made the move and hugged her. She responded. We kissed. We kissed. We kissed. We hugged. We hugged. We hugged. We touched each other's arms and legs and kissed and hugged. This went on for several hours, clothes intact. My parakeets were in their cage next to the sofa. Finally in the middle of the night, our clothes found their way to the floor. When they did, one of the birds chirped a wolf whistle. We laughed. Maybe he wasn't so dumb and was enjoying the show.

When Alba left the next morning, I felt good. I didn't feel madly in love, didn't feel I had to be with her every moment. I could say good-bye without separation anxiety. Ah, I'd finally learned how to be in a healthy relationship, I thought.

That was, of course, before the future brought with it Alba's yo-yo personality. She loves me, she loves me not, began having meaning for me. I started getting anxious.

We had exchanged "I love you" but it had taken a long time. Alba said she hadn't wanted to utter those words until a special moment. I'd wondered when the special moment was ever going to occur. But once it did, she told me three times in an hour or so. I was elated.

However, the yo-yo syndrome continued. The night came when she nearly gave me a cardiac, saying she still had feelings for her ex-fiancé Robert. *What??* She had told me that they were just friends. She said...she said...she said...But what did any of it mean? I was in love. I wanted to spend my life with Alba. Now I didn't know if I'd spend another day with her. I thought I'd die, but I remained calm.

The relationship continued and she was glad that I hung in there with her. The only problem was–I stopped trusting her. Any time her phone was busy, I wondered if it was *him*. Any time she said she couldn't get together or was seeing a friend, I thought it was *him*. At the same time, she told me how important it was that I trust her. So, though my guts said, "Don't! You're about to get massacred!" I continued seeing her and trying to trust her. (How does someone *try* to trust someone?)

I got into therapy. I wrote in my journal. I went to support groups. I played softball. But I tried to do these activities when I knew she was in school. God forbid I might miss a phone call. One night I was making myself dinner when Alba called to say she couldn't get her car started. I dropped everything and drove 20 miles to pick her up. In my excitement to be there when she needed me, I forgot the potato baking in the oven. It was not a pretty sight when I arrived home.

Was I obsessed? Yes. I hadn't been. But once I feared losing her, I became crazed. At the same time, I didn't want her to know I was crazed. That would really frighten her away. It was a familiar pattern. I'd gotten involved with someone with whom I was afraid to share my feelings.

By the time I was reporting my messes to my therapist every week, I was a mess. I was petrified, depressed, anxiety-ridden, irritable. My therapist thought Alba's yo-yo syndrome was from her school pressures. I hoped so. After all, we were most likely going to live together after school finished. That's what she said, at least. I started taking anti-depressants.

But as graduation approached, Alba became more distant. And once school finished, she went to New York to look for work, then to Minnesota to visit relatives. She arrived back home on Christmas Eve. By that time, the anti-depressants were alleviating some emotional pain, but I had physical pain. I'd always heard that one side effect of such medication was constipation. But I didn't know how severe a problem that could cause. I had a stabbing pain, as if by a hot branding iron, every time I attempted to go to the bathroom. It was the worst pain I had ever experienced in my life.

Alba returned from her trip. I picked her up at the airport. I always wanted to, always did. Part of being madly in love. We spent Christmas Eve and Christmas morning together, and made plans to attend a special service on New Year's Eve and then go to the Rose Parade on New Year's Day.

Things were actually going better when she called me in late December. "I have bad news for you," she began. "Robert wants me to go skiing with him for his birthday." She sounded so apologetic, as if it were something she couldn't do anything about. Robert supposedly had a girlfriend and I didn't for a moment believe Alba was Robert's second choice. I also questioned there really being a girlfriend.

I yelled and cried like never before with her. But in the end, Alba went skiing with Robert. I think I went into emotional low gear in order to survive. It was Mayday for me. Thank God I got angry. I considered taking all her stuff at my place and leaving it on her parents' porch. But, no, I hadn't enough pain yet. Maybe I was being clutchy. Maybe I was asking too much. Maybe if I were honest with myself and smelled the coffee, I wouldn't have been able to stand the pain of knowing she didn't want me.

Alba didn't love me. Or, if she did, she didn't want to. Surprisingly, we had a very good talk on her return, Alba saying she didn't feel able to commit. I was relieved she'd thrown up since the moment she and Robert arrived at the lodge. Of course, I showed interest in her health. I wasn't about to exalt, "Thank God you didn't have a chance to have sex with Robert! I'm glad you were puking all over!"

So we went to the New Year's Eve service and she told me how much better she felt that there was no longer a commitment. I aged 20 years when I really heard those words. But I wouldn't tell her. Hey, if she felt better without a commitment, we might spend the rest of our lives together. As long as she felt there was no commitment, she felt safe.

That seemed to make our relationship better for awhile, even though she wasn't physical with me. I was satisfied to be the person she called to do things together and to sleep with, even if all we did was sleep.

But Alba got a job out of state. She moved to Seattle and my phone bill became my highest bill after rent. Keeping contact was the way I alleviated pain, as well as going to therapy and talking about her, or seeing friends I'd stopped seeing and talking about her. All the while, I knew I was not taking care of myself. I was like a junkie that alleviates craving by having another dose of the killer drug. Contact with Alba, either by phone, letters or talking to others about her, was my fix.

This continued a few months until I learned that the problem created by the anti-depressants was going to require surgery. I had a hole torn inside me and it wasn't healing.

I called Alba and told her, looking for sympathy. She gave me a little and said she'd call the night of the operation. Thinking that I didn't want to go into the operation filled with resentment, I called Robert to clear the air. I had his number because Alba had written it down in my apartment when she'd called him from my place.

Well...Robert and I spoke for three hours. All was going well, both of us sharing our pain of our loss of the same woman, when he volunteered the information that they had had sex on that skiing trip, as well as a few other times during the time she was with me. I fell over backwards when he told me that. We hadn't had a commitment, but Alba and I had agreed we wouldn't sleep with anyone else. Robert also told me Alba was selfish, wanted things she couldn't have, was "dead in bed," and that he should have taken his girlfriend on that trip. I asked him not to tell Alba of our conversation until after I spoke with her. He said he wouldn't.

Alba called the night before my surgery. There was hesitation in her voice, so I asked if she had spoken to Robert. She had. Shit! He couldn't keep his mouth shut. Alba was very angry with me, saying she never wanted me to call Robert again and that he was very upset. *He* was upset?! What about me? Never once did she say anything like "I'm sorry." That would have been too much for someone with as much pride as she had. She did say she'd call after the operation to see how I was. I didn't tell her the things Robert said about her. She believed he was the only person she could trust. Based on her behavior and attitude, she would never have believed he said what he did.

I had the operation. I sobbed when I awakened from the anesthesia, and I had continuous dry heaves. A polyp was found in my colon, possibly pre-cancerous. I'd have to undergo another procedure to have it removed in the future. Terrific. Alba never called. Should I have been surprised? *She* was the pain in my ass.

At this point, I became as severely depressed as I'd been a few months before. I went to group therapy several times a day. I spent more time with a good friend of mine and I visited the neighbors downstairs until the early morning hours, playing games. I just couldn't sleep. I ate a lot, but I lost 10 pounds. I got involved in a metaphysical church. The minister began a newspaper and I wrote for it. I could write on just about any topic.

I took the opportunity to write a story called *Anger Must Come Before Forgiveness*. It was a parody of my relationship with Alba; I sent her a copy. I wasn't sure if I were being too cruel, but when one friend said Alba deserved it, I had to agree.

Yet the depression hung on quite awhile. I wasn't involved with sports, I wasn't taking classes, and I was unemployed. I don't know who would have hired me in the state of mind I was in.

I continued in therapy for months, finding psychodrama most effective. Whether acting out my pain or participating in that of another, feelings were expressed and I felt better about myself and much more alive.

The day came when I felt I was stuck, however, and decided I must see Alba and find out what happened. I drove to Seattle and surprised the hell out of her when she saw me. I'd hoped for a hug and sudden forgiveness all around. Dream on. She reluctantly had lunch with me, where I learned she was living with a woman. She'd found Ms. Right. All the warnings of my friends not to take this trip rang in my ears. I didn't act upset, but I felt like I'd died again. I stayed with friends for two weeks, exploring the city and having some fun. I kept the hope that I'd see Alba again before I left, but she refused to see me when I called. She ended the phone call quickly. I've never drunk coffee, but I finally smelled it: she didn't want me for a lover, she didn't want me for a friend. (And she wasn't wild about the story I'd sent her.)

I crawled back to my home near San Francisco. I realized I had to let go of Alba and go on. I went to singles groups and other lesbian activities. I began art classes to learn how to create sculptures and paintings. I built a bookcase. I got involved in a church that felt supportive of my values. I did volunteer work for a congressional politician's campaign.

The day came when I didn't want Alba anymore. I wanted to be free of the chains I had put on myself. I didn't want to spend my life wondering what Alba was doing and with whom. I didn't want to spend more money on tarot readers to tell me if Alba and I were ever going to be together again.

I learned that Alba and "Ms. Right" broke up after several months. I'd compared myself with Robert and Ms. Right, torturing myself with thoughts that something was wrong with me. But the only thing wrong with me was that I'd let Alba run my life. No wonder she lost her attraction to me.

But that didn't give her the right to mistreat me with behavior I took because I convinced myself that she just needed someone she could trust. I'd overlooked the double messages and never said, "Enough is enough." I'd been so afraid of being left that I stayed in a relationship where I went through emotional acrobatics while waiting for Alba to become consistent.

Early in our relationship, Alba and I had a joke about a song entitled *Always and Forever*. It seemed young lovers called a certain radio station and requested that song more than any other. The joke lost its humor. But through the pain, I think I'll always and forever never put myself through that kind of relationship again. Life is too short.

I've been hurt so much by women that I feel like trying a man sometimes. I know a man can't hurt me like a woman can. I just can't take it anymore, but I don't want to be alone, either. Am I crazy or is this a viable solution?

This statement or consideration about being with a man is not uncommon among Lesbians who have been hurt by a woman in a relationship. What's odd is that you don't hear "straight" women who get hurt by men saying, "I'll try a woman. I know a woman can't hurt me like a man." We need to recognize that loving, caring and being involved with another human being, a woman with a woman, is not easily given up. Lesbian relationships fulfill many emotional, spiritual, sexual needs that you can feel terribly disappointed about if the relationship doesn't work out. Could it be that you want to dismiss your feelings in a way from the pain and not deal with finding better ways of coping in a more productive manner with a woman the next time?

Shadows in the Mirror
by Randy Turoff

It's hard to become more than the conglomeration of your own disasters, yours and theirs. But once you see it, so they say, you're never the same. This intense swirling in my stomach, a kind of nausea, keeps repeating itself. The fears keep coming back and that feeling again of losing center, losing control, keeps pulling me down under. This artifice of sanity is built on quicksand.

I'm walking through this saltwater lake, picking up sea junk which is adhering to me. Sea burrs embedded in my flesh. On the bottom of the lake there are painful crab stingers which prick me. The stingers prick and then long white worms, like maggots, bore out of the soles of my feet.

I feel as though I'm in a movie, but the pain is real. A voice-over is narrating: "Everyone has stuff. The lake is full of unfinished stuff. Everyone is subjected to the stuff in the lake. We all have our stories of sex, duplicity and death."

A Huichol map of the Beyond shows souls unburdening themselves of their sexual attachments, in the shapes of the genitals of their former lovers.

A man sidles up, his hardness is up against the child who feels it but doesn't say anything. She feels the sensation of feeling it. The man is her father. She told me how her sister was passed among her father's friends until he institutionalized her.

I'm remembering what I went through with her. What I went through. Me, her, it was so much the same. Like the figure-eight, I never knew where she ended and where I began. Our lovemaking was like that. It was perfect and inexhaustible. All night, all morning, and half the next day. Before two sentences had ever passed between us, we encountered each other for the first time and spent it together in total ecstasy. The relationship was as-if real, indirect, a product of moonlight. She never knew me, I never knew her, but we were connected to the same tide, pulling us together like gravity. We communicated strictly through innuendo, lightning quick signals, subliminal chemistry. When I touched her, my fingers burst into flame. There was no solidity to us, no continuity, no friendship. The relationship was as unreliable as an hallucination. It was only when she held me in her arms, and I felt the fire between us, that I could be sure I wasn't imagining this other person, this phantom lover, this flitting ghost.

Our relationship was a spiral dance. Sometimes, on the outer edge, we were far apart, sometimes we were in perigee. But our orbits were reflective, we even menstruated in precisely the same cycle. The spiral nature of the relationship made it feel cosmic. It was a spiral dance of death. The center was utterly hollow, and every time we came close, we skirted the abyss. I believed from that start that L...was something karmic for me. It took me a longer time to realize the magnitude, the intensity of that truth. When L...plunged down into the abyss, I followed her. Not only was I incapable of helping her, but I got stuck there myself and it was my own living hell.

The stage is black. The moon is full and wicked in Scorpio. The stage is set for sexual cruelty. The curtains are dripping plush red blood. Every image is heightened. The primal drama is played out again and again, in fragments, in nightmares, in sensations without meaning. The orphan soul is cast adrift in the night and raped by demons. The child has no self and she doesn't even know what there is to protect. They always enter first through the eyes, because they can see this child has no self, and violation is as easy as jelly. The man sidles up, his hardness against the child who feels it but doesn't say anything. She feels the sensation of feeling it.

Under the blankets, in the darkness where boundaries dissolve, she kept having feelings. Memories coming up with the smell of unaired things. Obscure things, shadowy things, things that smelled like stale sex, or a stagnant swamp. Sometimes it was only the weight and burden of it that she felt. The heaviness of her life. The deep and heavy depression. The feeling of living on the bottom of a cesspool beneath so much shit she couldn't even imagine sunlight. She'd become a total eclipse of herself.

She lived inside her mind, in a back room, huddled in a dark closet where she felt protected. And she was protected, but not from her own mind. The defensive strategy worked except for the isolation, the drama of every outside encounter, the utter fear of closeness. The unhappy child grew into a hypersensitive and heavily armored adult. Oddly enough, sex became her escape into life. It was how she came to know other people outside of her mind.

At least, that's my theory. She watched me as if through a net. I could see her, but I could never really get close. She reached out if she needed something from me, but I wasn't allowed in. In fact, the more energy I poured into loving her, the more drained I became. The love wasn't nurtured or given a chance to grow. It was like pouring energy into a bottomless vessel or planting seeds in hostile terrain. There is no blame here, I chose to continue a futile effort through my ignorance. I mistakenly believed that my love could heal her.

The crazy drama with L...began to represent something extremely important to me. The greater my need became to love her, as incapable as she was of loving me, the greater my need to love myself. As we mirrored each other in passion, so we mirrored each other in pain. Whatever I had been blind to in myself, I indirectly saw reflected in her. Either we really *were* so much alike, or else she was the perfect vehicle for the projection.

As much as we couldn't get enough of each other in bed, that's as much as we tormented each other even after we had stopped having sex together. We'd always run into each other and the obsession had as much energy to it as did the passion.

If I were with somebody, she'd stare at me all night, watching every gesture, every movement, every beat of my heart. And if she weren't doing it to me, I'd be doing it to her. If mutual acquaintances were around, she'd act as if she hardly knew me. I began to dread going places.

After the first major separation, about three months, I found myself at a party where there were hundreds of women. The minute I entered the house, I felt her presence ripple through me. My body was an antenna for her vibrations. I tried to avoid her, but we ended up on the dance floor without anything but a nervous "Hi" between us. The floor was packed, and I was doing my own little dance, hardly looking at her at all. She managed to keep her eyes closed through most of it. Halfway through the number, I suddenly lost my balance with a jolt, and I realized she and I were coming together, like rapid firing back/forth, back/forth, and back and forth, and I was shocked and humiliated at my body for responding so completely to hers.

This chance meeting set off another flurry of activity between us. At first I deliberately downplayed my feelings, but I underestimated the extent of the addiction. Any sharing of joy that once existed had already outlived itself and had turned into a painful stasis. Every time I saw her, I'd come home feeling depleted, as if my very life force had been sucked dry. It was as if she had been feeding off me. "I'd die without you," that old romantic standby, had taken a vengeful turn. The delusions of romance had sent their henchman after me when I was at my weakest. My willpower was practically nil.

Buddhists believe that we choose the wombs through which we will be reborn. Choosing a lover, not just a girlfriend, but a lover, is like choosing a mother. Whatever we haven't worked out, we will be obliged to work out. We choose the lovers who inadvertently fit the patterns of our karma. Psychologists trace the pattern back to the stuff you've never worked out with your family mother. Buddhists go back further to many past life connections with many mothers. And all the mothers are also children, frightened and insecure. You can ask yourself: "Will I be rejected by the womb I chose to enter? Will my attempts to love be aborted? Will this woman be able to love me beyond her own narcissism, to treat me as something within and beyond her own stuff?"

L...was not a very wise choice for me. Sometimes one has to confront death for one's revelations. Passion is dramatic. The goddesses of creation have their terrifying destructive sides. The goddesses of passion are mighty, awesome creatures before whom you tremble in submission. Passionate relationships may be merely mortal, but they do make mythic dramas of our projections. Perhaps we do attract the actresses to the roles we are creating from our own fantasies. Perhaps each of us is there to act out the roles in each others' primal drama. I don't know. Why do we relish keeping each other as objects of forbidden fascination? Why do we keep treating each other as stage personae, limiting each other to the sexual roles of our fantasies? Is this simply the price we must pay for passion?

I haven't seen or heard from or asked after L...in several months. I travel in different circles now. I'm not a prisoner of the script anymore. I stopped acting out the drama. It's a strange, Pirandello-like feeling. It's as if the actor suddenly left the stage in the midst of performance and simply took a seat in the audience. The actor merely broke the 4th wall and in so doing, the drama ceases to exist. The other actors leave the stage through the wings. The audience becomes quickly bored and goes home. Only the critic remains, shuffling through a pad of random notes, re-arranging the fragments, and wondering on paper, what was all that really about?

Moving on—Making Peace
by Isabel De Maris

W hen a fantasy ends or a lifeline breaks, loss is not always immediately obvious. Denial pulls a thick curtain over reality. Life goes on. Workaholism kicks in. Keep moving. Try a new angle, a new direction. All problems can be worked out, can't they?

But, when time inevitably wakes the sleeping mind, the pain of loss denied can be almost too strong to bear.

My relationship with Gail lasted nine years. She was my first lover, and in many ways, my first friend. Our joining together was a classic story for that cocktail party question, "How did you meet?"

Gail and I fell in love at summer camp when we were both fifteen. For two years we faithfully wrote weekly (sometimes daily) love letters from our separate homes. From the strong, separatist community of East Lansing, Michigan, Gail was able to envision a dream of us being together one day. And in my closeted Connecticut town, I clung to that dream.

Through more or less independent planning, we ended up at the same university. Gail was pre-med and I was a music major. We lived together throughout college, spent our senior year together in Japan, returned to the States, and lived together for two years in a group home in Boston.

To our single friends, we were known as "that old married couple." We were consistent, committed and stable when nearly everyone else we know was floundering. We grew up together and came out together. We shared the frustrations of career choice and the struggles of school. We experienced exotic and adventurous travels and the relative freedoms of a post-graduation life in the suburbs. Gail was my support and friend, and I was hers. We knew each other's weaknesses and took care of each other. I thought we would be together forever.

It's difficult to think about the year that ended my relationship with Gail. A heavy emotional pile of guilt, sadness, frustration, embarrassment and anger overwhelms me when I try to make sense of our separation. Though I have sometimes felt a wonderful spirit awakening in my life apart from her, I am also haunted by a fear that a beautiful relationship died needlessly.

Gail left me for another woman. Sex was part of our problem: I suffered from a lack of interest in orgasm, due mostly to bottled up life frustration, confusion and depression. Gail longed to know she could fulfill me sexually. Unfortunately, we never really dealt with the difficult issues; both she and I denied our frustrations. I also denied there was a problem, even after Gail had told me she was falling in love with someone else and that they had slept together. Somehow, I thought that a little sexual variety for Gail might ease the tensions in our relationship.

On some basic level, I took our love for granted. Because we had been such primary support for each other during a very difficult adolescence (because of our love, my family pushed me away and Gail pushed away her own), I believed we would survive any and all of life's struggles.

My immediate response to Gail's news that she had slept with someone else was a feeling that I needed to meet this woman and make her a part of my life. It is with embarrassment, then, that I look back on a year spent opening doors, opening my heart, sharing my fears and dreams, compromising, working out agreements, playing football and basketball, becoming friends and almost falling in love with the woman who would eventually lead Gail out of my life. The year was impulsive and reactionary, but it really felt no stranger than the crazy path of love I had already followed in life.

Reality eventually set in, and it became apparent that Gail and her lover did not share my utopian, open-marriage fantasy. Gail and I took separate bedrooms less than a month before she moved out. The last time we made love (and I remember really enjoying it) was the evening before we slept in separate rooms for the first time in seven years.

Hurt and angry, I found myself attracted to a supportive, straight woman I worked with. I soon discovered the attraction was mutual, and in a spiteful act of revenge, I loudly seduced her from my separate bedroom. My sexuality was suddenly alive. Gail moved out of the house within a week.

My struggle to overcome loss has been enormously difficult. When I lost Gail, I lost my faith in love.

In the first few weeks after we separated, I was numb, but couldn't eat or sleep without sobbing. I felt as if my world and sense of sanity had been raped. I just hadn't seen the end approaching.

My friends were supportive, but I was too proud and hurt to speak much with them. I couldn't discuss my lesbian divorce at work. My family, who after several years of rejection had come to accept my relationship with Gail, took the news of our breakup very casually, almost as though they were relieved.

In an ultimate act of survival and denial, I immediately pursued a relationship with my new woman friend. She was receptive, but very confused. Our tidal wave romance lasted almost a year before she decided she could not live self-identified as a bisexual. I turned my psyche inside out trying to keep up on an emotional racetrack of falling in love and mourning.

I finally admitted I needed professional help when I realized I felt furious at my new lover because she could not give me back the security I had once known with Gail. I called a therapist and have been grappling with my sadness ever since.

I have been able to "get over" my relationship with Gail. Over the years, I have alternately made peace with Gail, gotten angry, apologize, stayed friends, and drifted apart. I no longer allow myself to need her. When I think of her, I do not hate her. But I do not love her, either. I believe, on most levels, I understand her.

I have often speculated that Gail has not yet dealt with the pain that destroyed our love. Gail left me before beginning her work at medical school. She left me because it was the simplest way for her to start fresh as an adult without the obvious baggage of childhood. When we speak now, there is a distance. Though we talk of friendship, I do not believe we are friends. I cannot get close to her. I feel she must still harbor anger.

If Gail has avoided her pain, however, I have been forced to deal with mine, probably for the first time. I was the woman left standing. Gail was the woman empowered. I felt victimized, and facing my pain was a matter of survival.

The irony is, of course, that in exploring the pain and anger of lost love, I have also had to look honestly at the pain, anger and depression

I have known all my life. In recovering from childhood pain, it has become easier to weave sense into my breakup with Gail.

My childhood was spent alone. I was the youngest of five children, but with working parents I was left with a sitter at the age of three. With no other children to play with, I learned to entertain myself. I remember feeling sad and alone at that young age. The feeling has never really left me.

My mother was a "supermom" before it was fashionable. She taught school and returned home to gather up the kids and take care of the house. I believe she was brutally dissatisfied with her life. She always complained about the workload. Her kids were slobs, her husband didn't understand her, there was too little time to stop and enjoy life. Years later, when all her children had left the house, my mother retired early and became a fitness, fun and frivolity freak. It was almost scary to see her come to life.

I grew uncomfortable in social situations. I remember feeling like an outsider at the Christian nursery school and kindergarten where I was sent, partly because I didn't have a mom like the other kids, one who made them bacon and eggs for breakfast, worried about how they looked, picked them up right after school and read them Bible stories at night. I got sick on the way to school one day, and my mother got mad at me because she had to take me to work with her. I often felt my mother endured me more than loved me.

First grade was different. In a new school, I was near the top of my class and I was popular. I had a gang of friends who followed me around at recess. My teacher was warm and encouraging. My mother even came to Parent's Day.

But memories after first grade grow hazy. I had begun to sink into sadness. I was moved up to a new class and was no longer the star pupil. I began to feel social pressures for being a "tomboy."

My parents had my nearest sister join me at my school to simplify travel, and she resented the move for years. I think that may have been the beginning of a long-running rivalry between us. I also remember a growing jealousy of my nearest brother, who was able to play all the games I wanted to play without social stigma. My mother had grown very unhappy with the lack of social network in the small town where we lived. There was a lot of sadness in the house. I kept to myself. I think I cried every day.

When I was nine, we moved to a larger town. In trying to make friends at my new urban school, I found myself involved in several sexually exploitative situations with neighborhood boys. I never told my mother. While not violent, these episodes only served to increase my distrust of friends and men.

I felt outside the mainstream. As adolescence approached, my differences with other girls became more pronounced. When my grandfather died, my mother fell into a depression that, by her own admission, lasted several years. My father, who was consistent all his life, worked very hard for the family, but mostly kept to himself. Without a parent to pull us together, my siblings and I grew more and more distant. I convinced myself I was a loner and didn't need support.

Naturally, I couldn't deny my need for love forever. At thirteen, I spent my first summer at music camp and had my first real encounter with friendly peers and warm supportive adults. By the end of the summer I was hooked. Finding love became an obsession.

In my child's mind, I couldn't understand denial. I could neither recognize my past denial of love nor my sudden crushing obsession to find it. For two more years I floundered in a lonely fog of confusion, longing and desperate searching for some nebulous feeling of warmth and support. I had constant fantasies of adult women teachers, church leaders or camp counselors holding me in their arms. I lost all passion for living. My schoolwork suffered, but because I had already been tracked as an intelligent student, no one seemed to notice. As a troubled child, I fell through the cracks.

The key to my obsessive love for Gail lies in my sad childhood. When we finally met and our passions clicked so immediately and deeply, her love was the answer to my prayers. I clung to my belief in the permanence of that love, even after we had begun to struggle as a couple. I gave up my study of music early on. Instead, I chose a major that put less time pressure on our relationship. Gail made sacrifices of her own. We made choices as a couple that probably were not in our best interest as individuals. But for our separate reasons, the need for security and love was primary.

Sometimes I look back on our breakup with rage. Today I want to tell Gail, "You treated me like dog shit! You stepped on me, cursed me and scraped me away. You blamed our relationship for all your weaknesses and ran in order to deal with them. I was not the root of your problems. Gail, I felt so much love for you. I deserved better treatment."

It's been three years since we broke up. I am only now making peace with myself. In spite of my anger, I can look back on my relationship with Gail without regret. We helped each other through some difficult years. I'm glad she was there when I was younger and needed her, but I am an adult now. I have the control I need to make my life happy.

I have started playing my music again. I have begun to look at career choices I can make for my own fulfillment. I am finding belief in myself, in my ability to be loved and to give love without giving away my soul. I trust friendship again and also am beginning to trust friendship with men. I am also making peace with my family. My father's sudden death a year ago brought together my siblings as adults. We have become friends, somehow sensing our mortality and our need to support each other. My growing friendship with the brother and sister I competed with as a child has been one of the greatest contributors to my recovery. It has allowed me to let go of the past.

My recovery is not over. I often feel frustration and wonder if I will ever be "cured" of my sadness. My hope is that I have recognized the enemy. Denial has made my pain unbearable. When I feel sadness, or loneliness or anger, if I face my emotions I can reach out and deal with them. It is the lesson of recovery that I never want to forget.

Peace Camp Summer
by Ginny Foster

In 1983, Sandra Jo left to visit the Women's Peace Camp near Seattle. She fell into an engrossing and exciting way of life. We'd set up a contract beforehand to live together again and get counseling if we felt we were losing our relationship. But that was soon disregarded. Initially I retained faith that our contract would be respected, but not after I visited the camp and saw her physical affection with other women. I became more disillusioned after discovering Sandra Jo was sleeping with other women. I was sad and bitter. I told her I didn't want to continue visiting each other unless she could be monogamous.

I'd begun a daily journal that year. At the time, I didn't realize that it would become a chronicle of the breakup with my lover of five years.

June 6, 1983
Sandra just went through the kitchen and said, "I like my life with you, Ginny." I like it, too. Sandra conducted and facilitated the process of evaluation and got the agenda started for the next meeting of the women's peace networking meeting. Between set up and the start at seven, I walked to the store and sat against the wall. Needed the time out.

June 10
I raised my voice when telling Sandra Jo one more time that I was going to stay home tonight instead of going to the Quaker Gay Potluck. I said "have a good time" and Sandra Jo said "I'd have a better time if

you were going." This gives me an idea for an article on GLOMMING (to each other). I have to make sure I have enough space.

June 13

Sandra Jo said this was a perfect day at the cabin. Making love was so slow and wonderful, both for her and me. I like walking alone and she likes walking fast. The perfect solution to the Glom Factor...walk separately, which we did.

June 18

Today the Peace Camp opened in Kent, near Seattle. Every place we go I take their leaflets in my backpack and put them up. Sandra Jo said "I'm tired of that crap." I felt like she was putting down my work as not valuable and I told her so. I feel that getting the word out is as important as going to meetings.

June 20

After Gay Pride, Sandra Jo stayed four hours talking at Old Wives Tales Restaurant. I was beat. It rained. I had to protect the literature. Sandra's teenage son Brett knocked four times on my closed door for one thing or another, so I finally asked him not to talk to me at all.

June 21

I woke up in touch with what I want: 1) I don't want Sandra Jo to interfere, to defend and rescue Brett when he and I are arguing. He's 17 years old. 2) I don't want to go to the work party at the cabin. Boring talk. 3) I don't want to go on our trip to Washington (state). Brett will be back East and I want to be in my home alone. Now what am I going to do???

June 22

Big fight. She's afraid my attitude is damaging Brett. I need more time alone. I wonder if people have fights so they can have some space apart.

June 26

I'm home alone. I just want to have control of my own life. I feel caught in a web of relationships. I imagine myself writing, organizing my papers, but even if I'd just read all the time or sit and look out the window it would be okay. I just want to be free. Freedom is my highest value.

Sandra Jo must have gotten to the peace camp today. Will I wonder what I'm missing? "No regrets," I always say.

From Letters to Sandra Jo in Early July

Your pillow is lonesome but dauntless...

Darling, what can I say to you? The best we can do is to make our diverging (temporarily) frames of reference be the source of excitement and sharing when we once more come together. All your neighbors and friends ask about you and your lover thinks about you but is content.

July 20

I visited the Peace Camp, but I could not stay more than two days because I'm not the Hippie-Girl Scout-Revolutionary Camp type. I couldn't sleep, lying awake problem-solving about the lack of sanitation and nutrition...and politics.

July 27

Just talked to S.J. She's unhappy because I'm not "sharing my emotions." Shit, I've written her every day and made two trips up there and she hasn't written me in weeks or come to visit. So why does she have the right to be mad at me?

I don't want to be stirred up. I feel a quiet joy most of the time.

Sandra Jo wanted me to come to Bellingham to a meeting she's going to. There is something in me that likes being alone. She said she meant "intimacy" was missing from my letters. Her letters were just missing. I *like* having my life run on an even keel without a lot of emotional brou-ha-ha.

We went to our cabin on Mt. Hood for her birthday.

Birthday Wishes
may the spirit of gentle resistance
be with you this year
may we be found
at peace in the world together
in whatever weird way
we can arrange it

may we walk across the Bridge of the Ring
and from the Y walk up Still Creek Road
past the Monstrous Lichen on the stump
with the leaning Power Poles on the right
and the stones of the Dried-Up Creek on the left
may we pick mint together
all the summers to come
and crushing its leaves between thumb and forefinger
smell the same essence in perfect communication
both sharing the same sensation at the same time

may all our hands and thoughts
turn to that ball of clay
we call the earth
and the graffiti
we call the present
as we shape the future
one that can contain the yielding water
a vessel worthy for our lives

September 2
I settled into a new apartment.

September 26
Letter to Sandra:
I see a lot in my journal about times I was alone in the house and loved it. So maybe I was subliminally halfway responsible for our decision, to live apart, although that is very hard to convey to friends and sometimes hard to admit to myself...

I wonder if we'll ever live together again. I wonder if I will ever live with *anybody* again. What would be ideal for me is if you were down the hall.

I need your address. However, if I don't get a letter tomorrow from you, I may *not* need your address.

I'd love you if you were here. Do you still exist? Was it all a dream?

Early October
Letter to Sandra:
You'll be here in a week and a day and I am wildly looking forward to kissing you and making love, but above all, talking.

October 6
Sandra coming tomorrow. In my thoughts. Thinking about mail. Want a letter from Sandra.

October 9
After she went out, I lay on the floor and sobbed, "Why did you leave me?"

October 14
Sandra left today. The love letter from Diane she kept hurt me. I said to her at the train station that if she loved me she wouldn't sleep with Diane.

It's hard not to be bitter about all women when one treats you as a man would. She doesn't want entanglement, commitment, marriage. She wants to be free but still able to come down here and fuck me...fuck 'em and leave 'em just like a man.

My conditions:
1)Live in the same town
2)Be monogamous.
I don't want to go to Seattle...be totally dependent on her for companionship, etc., or, on the other hand, not see each other.
How does one live through anguish and still celebrate love?

Letter to Sandra Jo:
I realized walking home from the train station, crying, that I had been practicing denial again, pretending that you and I were really back together, or could be...

I cannot tell you how much it hurts me to think of you making love with someone else, that private act we shared.

I feel unequal: I feel like I love you much more than you love me and I'm not willing to continue to see you on an unequal basis. So until I get to loving you less, until we can meet as equals—I want not to see you......

However, I want to give our relationship every chance. Perhaps I am mistaken. Perhaps you really love me. If you are willing to be monogamous and to consider the Peace Camp your job and live with me, I would take that as a real sign of your love. I would be willing to trust you enough to come to Kent or Seattle to live, or you here.

If not, I don't want to invest any more time in you. I want to use my energy to find someone else and try to either catch the brass ring again or to learn to live alone and commit myself to my writing.

So don't plan on staying with me unless you are willing to make some kind of commitment, other than that of visiting tourist.

October 16
How do I get over thinking "is she the one who will take S.J.'s place?" about every woman I go out with?

October 17
S.J. doesn't even save my letters and I'm a writer!

October 20
Fantasies of vengeance. A collage of her statements and agreement contract with LIAR written across. Hate letters to Diane, the peace camp woman she's sleeping with.

What kind of sisterhood is it? Before I often found myself in conflict with some other woman over a man. And now I find the same thing is true. A woman has slept with my partner, not that I let my partner off the hook.

I'm face to face with my ego. I'm jealous. I haven't seen Sandra cry once over this. Cold bitch. How can I get over loving her so much? She is in my consciousness.

No wonder others don't take gay relationships seriously. Despite her being a Quaker, we broke up without going before the clearness committee the way another couple would.

Love is an illusion, a game. The dominant myth of our time. We had a contract to live together again and get counseling before we would consider breaking up.

October 21
Sandra was here when I got back. She said "I love you but I don't want to marry you." I said "Does that mean you won't live in the same

house or be monogamous?" She said "Yes." I said "Give me my keys." She fumbled. I grabbed them so hard it knocked off her glasses. I took them and said "Get out and don't try to see me again."

I have no moral compunction. I couldn't sleep, drank half a bottle of wine. Went downtown this morning and withdrew the $230 from our joint account. Went directly to the phone company and paid to have a phone installed. I feel no need to be honorable. She didn't honor our contract.

I sent some dishonorable cards to her, saying that I intended to rip up her clothes and papers she had stored with me. Eventually I took her papers and family pictures up to her cabin on Mt. Hood and left them. I sent a card. "You have hurt me more than any man ever did, because I trusted you more."

I feel better. After kicking, pounding pillows, screaming and crying last night. Now I feel it's over. The phone is symbolic of my new life.

October 22

I am doing some very deep emotional work. Like primal scream, and it's scary because I'm doing it all alone–no therapist. Crying, saying "I'm all alone." "She's dead."

Jacqueline and Marguerite and Sandy and I eating Chinese food. I get by with a little help from my friends.

Is she mourning the loss of our love at all? It seems like she is not feeling anything but an excitement over her own power in a group.

the first few minutes
I wake up and start to leap to the day
before I remember you have left
and I feel the weight in my stomach
that keeps me lying prone
on the bed

I said I liked being alone sometimes
be careful what you ask for
you may get it

I am determined not to short-circuit my freak-out
because if I can't love your Revolution
I don't want to come

these are the stages of loss of love:
denial
hurt
anger
I don't know what's coming next

it's like surfing
to go from one to the next
the risk of drowning

lying in the bathtub
letting the water's warm loving arms
enfold me

for a moment I do not think of you.

October 23
Letter to Sandra Jo:
　　Rationally and intellectually I understand your need to be free, but emotionally my feelings are hurt and abandonment.
　　One thing I've thought is how casually you broke it up. You expect the Quakers to take gay relationships seriously, but you didn't, for instance, call for a Clearness committee or abide by our contract to try to resolve differences in transition. I feel like I've been treated like Kleenex—the disposable society of love.

October 24
　　Some ethical dilemmas here:
You are not responsible for my feelings
vs. I feel hurt
The selfishness of thinking of what one wants for herself
vs. being a warm, caring person.
"Let there be peace in the world and let it begin with me"
vs. "expressing one's anger."

October 31
Western Union Telegram from Sandra Jo:
I too grieving our past relationship. You are most exciting woman I know. Love you. I want changing ways of sharing our lives.

November 4
Rather over-scheduled my birthday week to play out all the roles Sandra would have filled.

November 11
She called after taking stuff to cabin. I just cried and it was awful.

I love you like sugar; it's no good for me—don't call. I know I'm looking for a new lover because I bleached all my panties and bras.

January 20, 1984
From a letter to Sandra Jo:
I think if I saw you, I would either get mad or cry, so even if I always found your company interesting, I couldn't see risking that in the foreseeable future. (Foreseeable, a term which could mean anything from next spring to eons from now.) I spend a lot of time alone, by choice.

The journal ends here. I never saw Sandra Jo again. I had a few flings with other women, but my feeling that Sandra Jo had behaved "just like a man" meant I no longer felt women were superior to men in relationships.

The healing that occurred was not between Sandra Jo and myself, but with myself, sexually and creatively. I have learned to like contentment rather than melodrama. The healing was a reconciliation with my need for the freedom I find in solitude, not the same, but parallel, to the freedom Sandra Jo sought in other places and people.

I used to see my journal as the record of Sandra's betrayal. But I now realize the events were a gradual revelation to myself of my deepest longing...the solitude of living alone and writing. And that's what I now have.

On Velvet Paw

On velvet paw, she steals into my dreams
Agile, sleek, unannounced.
A break of a twig, a brush against the bush,
The earth barely detects the rustle of her leg
Before the storm of love lost.

—We broke up not because of what we had,
But because of what could not have been—

Senses stir within the private darkness, sleep.
The scent of her body, fragrant perfume
A fingertip away, I reach to touch the magic,
Heart-shaped leaves and vines that shield her step,
In the tangled jungles of night
When the world is dead,
Softly, she comes.

Hold back the sun!
Delay the advance of harsh light, and Reality.
Let her tease me once more,
Rejoining, dabbling, tormenting,
Withdrawn but not forgotten,
Though separated by countless people
    and daily chores,
Hundred, millions of breaths away,
Exists the whisper of ancient trees.
Now and then, she speaks, ever gently, ever firm,
On velvet paw, she steals into my dreams.

Sue McConnell-Celi

My ex-lover used to hit me and call me names. With a lot of support, I got out of that relationship and feel much better about myself. Months have passed and she's calling me, saying she's changed. I still love her and miss her terribly. How do I know if it's safe to see her again?

 I say it's great if your ex-lover recognized she needed professional help. But how many months of therapy and with who, as well as what kind of therapy, is important for you to know. Did she learn what her alternatives to being abusive are when she's upset? What did she learn about herself and her need to be violent or verbally abusive toward you, the person she loves?

It's very important for you to feel secure in having contact with your ex-lover, even though you love and miss her. Meeting with her and her therapist is one helpful step to aid you in feeling less afraid and determining what you will choose to do.

You can establish ground rules which she can agree to in the presence of her therapist. Rebuilding trust is the key to your feeling safe with her. It's up to your ex-lover to prove to you that she has changed her violent and abusive behavior. You both will need the assistance of a therapist who can help you through this period of rebuilding trust and safety. If you choose not to seek a therapist experienced in this area, I would suggest keeping a watchful stance for the next three to six months and keep your support network close by.

The familiar scenario of
    darkened room,
with your retreat in to the inner realm.

No poem tonight: pure reality

  This journalist of journeys:

(why do J feel incomplete as J have misplaced
my judgement known heart)? —

Js this routinized bliss, or, two individuals amiss
of what lover's know best?

(The brandy helps).

Jessica Fair Stevens

Journey Toward Myself
by Tighe Instone

The year was 1962. She was twenty years older than I was. I was twenty-two, and this was my first real relationship and my first real sexual experience. When I say 'real,' I mean that I had kissed and cuddled with men and women, and I had tried sex with a guy but found that experience unpleasant and distressing.

I was euphoric. This was the most wonderful, amazing, incredible thing that had ever happened to me. At last my life had a meaning and a purpose. She was the most wonderful, amazing, incredible person–the way she dressed, the way she moved, the way she talked, the things she said. She was so interesting, so self assured–and SHE loved me!!!

BUT...she was a Roman Catholic. Though she worried about our relationship, she could not penetrate my euphoria......oh, joy, oh rapture......NO-NO-NO ! It's ours-it's love–it's pure–not bad–not sinful-not forbidden. Loving is not wrong–it's ecstasy!

We were closeted. We were special, I thought. No one knew our secret except us and I promised NEVER to tell anyone. Oh how I loved her, adored her, worshipped her. This WAS heaven on earth.

BUT...she continued to worry about us sinning. She tried to resist...we mustn't–it's bad. No–No–No–it's ours–it's love–it's beautiful. We lived together and loved together. We drank an awful lot of alcohol and we thought no one in the world knew about us.

BUT...that wonderful, amazing, incredible euphoria could not compete with the church and the guilt. Her dilemma was our dilemma and, of course, there were consequences. I took an overdose of aspirin. I thought it would be lethal, but all it did was make my ears ring–for days.

It was like having a resident symphony orchestra in my head. I found myself in a psychiatric ward with locked doors and no handles on the taps. Hospital personnel told my Mum and Dad, who in turn said I'd caused a lot of trouble. They did not approve of my relationship and agreed with the doctors that it would be best if I went away to the mountains to a hospital for people recovering from addictions and nervous breakdowns.

As soon as I returned, I visited my lover. We went to bed together. BUT–she told me afterwards–it must cease. But it did not cease, and the more she tried to resist, the less I understood. She took me to her church where we both lit candles. I was fascinated by all the statues but apparently talked too loudly. She said she would have drowned me at birth if she had been my mother. The priest said it didn't matter–it was good that I was so interested in everything.

Her resistance gradually strengthened. One night she entertained some chaps from next door. I got awfully drunk and tried to make her jealous by flirting with them. She would not be drawn: I ended up in bed with one of them. After that we had a terrible row. She said she never wanted to see me again. I was grief-stricken and, I discovered later, pregnant. The year before, I'd felt the world was at my feet. I had danced on cloud nine and revelled in the joys of loving and being loved. Now it was all gone–she hated me, I hated myself, I hated my growing pregnant body. I hated my Mum and Dad and their constant disapproval. I hated the horrid world and its disapproval. I determined a final solution for myself–and this time I would not fail.

I was unconscious for three days. I would have died, but my mother, while playing bridge, had an overwhelming sense that something was wrong and discovered me before it was too late. Oh–how could I do this to them–after all they had done? After my baby was born I saw very little of my parents for many years. Having a baby was unforgivable enough–but to be keeping it! I was forbidden to take my child to their home.

This was a turning point. It removed the subtle and not-so-subtle control that my parents had hitherto exercised over me. I was naïve, ignorant and ill-equipped to take responsibility for myself let alone for another human being. I drank booze in gay bars and tried to convince myself and my friends that I was an okay person.

Relationships came and went and I fell in love again in a big way. I spent the next six years with a lover who ridiculed and humiliated me. I hung in there for the good moments, which gradually became less and less frequent. Our relationship was not completely unproductive, however. We both sold all our belongings to raise money for a deposit on a house. This was 1972, when inflation was rampant and special legislation had to be introduced to stop speculation on residential property. We renovated the house, sold it, and bought a farmlet. This provided financial security for the future.

But I extricated myself eventually. I was desperate, not needed, and my self-esteem was at rock bottom. This was another turning point and once again, I sought refuge in gay bars and endeavored to prove myself to myself and those about me. At that time, there were conflicts raging between bar dykes and lesbian feminists—I didn't really understand the issues, but I was there, boots and all! Then I got involved in personal growth and consciousness raising. In 1979, I was enraged by the exclusion of lesbians and gays from this country's Human Rights Commission legislation.

That catapulted me into political action. Our first ever Lesbian Pride March in 1980 was a nerve-wracking, but also affirming, experience. The more involved I became in lesbian politics, the more aware I became of my inability to comprehend the issues. Even when I did, I was unable to articulate them effectively. In 1981, I attended a university in an endeavor to gain confidence, understanding and the ability to express myself. I stopped drinking because I had begun to see how instrumental it was in maintaining oppression. I wanted to see a reality that wasn't so distorted and I didn't wish to kill any more of my precious brain cells.

March 1985 saw the introduction of the Homosexual Law Reform Bill and the mobilization of the "moral minority." A nationwide petition opposing the bill was launched and homophobia pervaded the media and invaded our homes. My rage knew no bounds. I became involved in the organization of support for the bill and opposition to the "moral minority's" campaign. I helped distribute pamphlets on the street and was spat at, physically assaulted by rugger buggers* and had to deal with yobbos** setting fire to my table of pamphlets.

BUT they could not shake my pride in my lesbian identity. These experiences only increased my determination to fight for our right to live and love as we please.

During those early years I tried to make sense of a world that did not make sense and I had limited tools to carry out the task. Freedom from parental recriminations while breaking barriers enabled me to discover myself and make decisions about who I wanted to be. Pride in my lesbian identity, fighting for lesbian rights and knowing that my experiences contributed to that fight lifted my self-esteem and I even started to like myself! I stopped believing that one day Ms. Right would show up and all my problems would vanish. I strove for self-sufficiency.

As I became able to care for myself I was able to love and trust another lesbian, and I was able to feel loved and trusted too. I was able to be a partner in a relationship based on strong principles and to feel the strength that such a relationship provides.

* *rugger buggers:* a term to describe the violent macho male attitude typical of rugby players in New Zealand.

** *yobbos:* a general term used to describe ignorant young men whose behavior is destructive and/or violent.

An Island

Hurt and rejection slid on comfortably
   like an old pair of slippers when you left last night.
The familiarity of my aloneness softened the heartache
   and the pain deep within my soul.
Voices in my head spoke loud and clear:
   "Return to your existence as a rock and an island,"
   they said.
"For an island never cries and a rock feels no pain."

The seduction of those words washed over me
   like a warm ocean wave.
My mind cried out for the necessity
   to no longer feel or struggle for intimacy.
Yet, from deep within the center of my self
   came gentle, steady whispers
   of the joy of loving and of being loved.

The exhiliration of cracking open the steel walls
   surrounding my heart,
     allowing another person to peek inside,
     wavered.

The freedom to choose to love and be loved in return
   is like a baby taking her first unsure steps.
Won't is be difficult to gather all these new pulsating
   energies
Of joy, feeling, aliveness, and love...
   shove them back behind that steel wall,
     carefully replace the seal,
       until another time when strength returns
To slowly open the doors again,
   allowing those energies to fully breathe?

Am I capable of returning to that state of numbness
  now that I've had a taste of actually feeling
    the joy and the love
As well as the pain and the anger?

To not see a beloved's eyes light up
  when I come into view,
To no longer share tender words of intimacy,
To not experience the joy of belonging
  or the quiet ecstasy of mutual nurturing.

These are the behaviors I could no longer yearn for
  should I choose to anethesize my heart.
To stifle the weak inner voice slowly gaining volume,
to subdue the desires to be with another human being,
to withdraw and stiffen when my body is touched
  or to not hear the loving words describing my beauty
    which I am slowly beginning to acknowledge.

All this will require extensive amounts of energy
  I'm not certain I have,
For I would no longer allow my self
  to be sustained and comforted by another.

Numbing the pain
  would surely be a welcome blessing.
But I am not ready
  to have it become a lifelong commitment.
For I was not meant to live in isolation
  on my journey through life.

                                        Patti Azevedo

I left my lover because I didn't think I loved her anymore. The relationship seemed stagnant and so did she. Now I'm miserable without her and think about getting together again, but I'm afraid of making promises I can't keep. I don't want to hurt her again. I'm so confused I don't want to do anything. What's wrong with me?

It sounds as if what's missing in this relationship is your certainty regarding your feelings for your lover. These feelings need to be explored more thoroughly. What is it you need from your lover that you're not receiving? What is it that attracted you to her in the beginning? What changed your feelings? I wonder what you consider stagnant. Relationships have a tone of contentment which can be seen as boring or stagnant. If that's what you're saying, then I'd suggest you consider looking at that part of the relationship you want changed and make the contribution to change it. Don't expect the relationship to be the same after you left. You broke some part of the bond. You're right to be concerned about hurting your lover again. You also need to know if this is a pattern for you.

Blackberries and the Dilemmas of Weed Whacking a.k.a. How to Become a "Box" and Live to Tell About It

by Michelle Bancroft

"Don't be afraid to experience your pain, for it is the seed from which your greater expansion grows..." Karen LaPuma

My Decision

We have to talk...You sigh in exasperation. How many times have you heard that from me? This time, however, it is different. This time I am not suggesting that we go away together for a weekend to try to reconnect. I am not begging you to go into couple's therapy one last time, nor even asking you what has been bothering you the past couple of days. This time, it is to say I have made the decision to leave you.

You don't seem to realize how serious I am. Your reaction sickens me. You agree that maybe it is time for me to be on my own. You say this as if I were your dependent, powerless child who now must leave your nest. You seem to overlook the fact that I am NOT that anymore. Your condescending attitude chafes me.

I have bled for "The Relationship," wanting so badly for it to "Work" that it had become an entity in and of itself. That entity ruled my life. I could not see your withdrawal and indifference to me. I could not see that I was not in love with you anymore. I only worked harder to restore what we once had. I cry uncontrollaby as I tell you this. As usual, you just listen, not understanding my pain, not dealing with what is happening to us. I feel my anger rise, but now I can only cry.

Our Agreement

Because of school, I cannot move for another ten months. We had made plans to relocate together, but now I will be moving alone. We decide the best thing to do is continue to live together until the time comes when I must move. We talk in depth of what we want in the coming months. We agree not to see other women until I have moved out of our home. We vow that we will have a friendly, loving, caring parting. We plan to continue to be part of each other's lives once my move is complete. You say you still love me and always will and that a lot can happen in ten months. I, however, know that nothing will change my decision.

My Preparation

I talk. I talk to my friends, I talk to my parents, I talk to my brother, I talk to my cat, I talk to my therapist, I talk to my guiding Goddess. I talk about my decision to leave, I talk about my fears, I talk about my excitement at having a new life and the terror that idea generates in me, I talk about my frustrations and my anger. I talk about you. I talk about being without you.

I have been in a state of limbo with you that is eating away at my soul. I vacillate between yearning for the past and wanting to get the hell out. In public, you treat me as your girlfriend–you hold my hand, kiss me. At home, we sleep in separate beds. I am reaching my breaking point.

The time of my leaving draws near. In one month I will no longer live here. I am longing to be in the mountains, as far away from this city as I can get. I follow my instinct and go camping. I feel like an animal, very primal as I go to the mountains to isolate myself, to lick my wounds, to heal. I now fully understand why domesticated animals go away to die in the woods. It's about reconnection to the universal mother.

I am in a valley at 8,000 feet. It is surrounded by snow-capped peaks. I hike for a while and find my place on a rock. I am astounded by the beauty. A herd of deer grazes a few feet away. They let me become part of them. The stream that winds through this valley is high and crisp in its coolness. The air is so pure it pierces my lungs as I breathe in deeply. I am home. This is my Goddess' cathedral–my place of worship. I feel more complete and whole than I ever have been. I am beginning to see how fragmented I had become–maybe always was.

Journal entry:

Here I sit staring at the stark whiteness which has become my life. For the last six years, I have drawn on that blank slate what I thought I wanted, what I thought we both wanted. I was wrong. I now sit alone, enveloped in white. I choose a pen and begin to draw anew. This time, as I draw, I find myself creating beauty only I can fully appreciate–never stopping to wonder if someone else will approve. As I draw, I am spinning a web that is slowly becoming MY life that is no longer entitled OUR life. The more color I add, the less stark, sterile and forbidding my canvas becomes. To my glorious surprise, I realize I have the courage to do this.

Your Betrayal

My anger at you sears my body. How could you, after all we talked about? We had made an agreement which I thought was sealed with our mutual respect, trust and the love we once shared. I was wrong. I kept asking you why. You would only have had to wait five days until I would be gone. That number is now implanted in the recesses of my mind. I had kept encouraging you to make new friends, separate from me and our relationship–I just never thought in a million years you would fall "in love" and fuck one of them. As crazy as it seems, I not only feel betrayed by you, but by the whole entire lesbian race!

I had actually convinced myself that we were above this typical dyke drama. I spent the first day in shock, after you told me. I could not cry, could not get angry, could not feel anything. I could only feel this huge, thick wall of stone encasing me once more. Never again, I vow, will you ever touch my heart.

We begin to talk. I ask why. You don't know. God, I hate you. Five days, just five days...you didn't have that much respect for me and our relationship to wait five days. One part of me doesn't even care, another part hurts. I trusted you so unconditionally, so completely. You have walked all over that and me. One part of me can't understand; this part wants to kill you, that part wants to kill her, another part just wants to let it all go.

Once again, I talk. My friends help me sort out my feelings, my hurt. I write, I yell, I cry, I meditate. I feel.

My Loss

Dear Tonya,

It was you who was there when I began my recovery process. It was you who was there when I began to feel the depths of my pain that was a result from childhood abuse. It was you who held me as I cried, huddled and terrified in your arms. It was you who listened to my countless denials of how, maybe, it wasn't that bad. It was your arms and body that shielded me from the blackness of depression. It was you who encouraged me to go back to school. It was you who became a conditioned safety response, a vessel of my healing.

What am I to do without you? Will I be able to handle this new pain, alone? Will I ever feel safe again? Hugs from loving friends and family do not help. I do not share that connection with them, only you. I pray for that connection to be broken as much as I pray for it to be restored.

My neediness for you terrifies me...

Michelle

My Anger

My rage feels like a huge molten mass–fire, lava, a meteorite. It is concentrated in its power and intensity. I am not the rage–it is an entity in and of itself. I want to hurl it at Tonya and watch her burn in the pain she has caused me. I know the time will come when I will be able to cast it out of my life, but right now I need its protection and warmth.

Dear Tonya,

What a fool I have been! I have been the perfect little wife right up until the end. Making sure your needs were being met, supporting you emotionally, buying your clothes, making your dinner, doing your laundry, anticipating your needs. How disgusting! You never deserved any of my attention. You took it for granted.

This woman is just another pawn in your game of denial. By distracting yourself in this way, you have planted the seeds of YOUR demise–NOT mine.

You are the biggest coward I have ever known. I have lost any and all respect for you. Denial rules your life as you immerse yourself in your sick triviality. I no longer know who you are. I was loving an illusion.

From the most wonderful person you will ever know
and whom you have lost forever,
   Michelle

My Move

Today I leave. I am exhausted emotionally and physically. Even empty, our house is alive with memories. Close friends say goodbye, hold me, hug me. I miss them already; I don't want to leave. I walk outside, camera in hand, and begin to take pictures. My gardenias that I loved so much are in full bloom. How many times would I arrange a full bouquet of them to fill our house with their beauty? Did you love them as much as I? There were days we spent digging and replanting the flowers in the back. Some days we floated around the pool together, or I watched you mow the lawn. They were days we loved each other. I say goodbye to it all.

My Aloneness

Night 1: As incredible as it seems, I am actually alone. My cat is asleep in front of me, a candle is burning, as is my favorite incense. I am healing. I strip and make love to myself. I feel sexy and powerful. My new life has begun. I am leaving everything behind. She is gone and I am free to grow. I am becoming complete. I am becoming everything. I am becoming whole.

Night 2: Friends are staying with me. I'm glad they're here. They try to make me laugh. They say what an uncaring bitch Tonya is and how she was never right for me and how I can do SO much better. What else are friends for, anyway?

We decide to go to Tahoe for dinner and to veg out in front of the video poker machines. On the drive up, one of them confiscates my Patsy Cline tape that I have been playing over and over. Maybe she has a point–I really *don't* want to be "Back in Baby's Arms."

Night 3: Tahoe is a mistake. The only times I'd been there were with Tonya. Her memory permeates the place. We'd been in love the times we'd gone there. I remember the rooms where we stayed, the restaurants we loved, the drives we took around the lake, where we won, where we lost. I'm not able to stop the stream of memories pouring from the corners of my mind. I sit "vegging out" as planned and can feel her presence beside me. I keep turning around to see if she's there. More than once, I think I see her. The pain has begun...

Journal entry:

I hurt so horribly much. When will this pain ever go away? My whole body, my skin, aches. I cannot move. I want her to hug me so badly. Every nerve in my body cries out for it. Yet I know who she is with, who she is hugging now. I am so painfully alone. I will never be the same. I miss her. A part of me has been amputated. I can no longer turn to her. She will never be there for me in the same way. I want her to love me again–I need her. I can't believe she is doing this. My body aches. I want it to stop.

Where is she? I need to hide...I don't know what to do with this pain.

Night 4: I can't sleep, I can't eat. I can't think straight. I walk around my new home, just staring at boxes that still need to be unpacked; boxes full of memories of us. Someone, something get me out of this! I go out to my backyard hoping to enjoy the cool night air, hoping to clear my mind. As I look around, this thought attacks me: Who's going to mow my lawn now and who will be there to whack my weeds???? I find myself crying uncontrollably once more. Will this ever end?

Journal entry:

I can't do this. I just want to go home. I want to curl up on her lap and be held. I need to see her. I am no longer welcome or wanted there. I hate it here! I don't belong here. I want to go home. I miss her. I need to hide. I know her fuck is in our bed as I write this. That bitch is getting what I want and need. I hate her!! I hate them!! WHY? Oh, please give me relief. The pain is too great. I am dying.

Night 5: OK, I do a stupid thing. I call Tonya. I just couldn't take it anymore. I have to hear her voice. I even ask her to come see me as soon as she can. I need her to make all this pain disappear. All I know is confusion. God, I'm bawling my eyes out on the phone. Of course, SHE is FINE. I don't know whether I miss her or the comfort and security she has represented to me all these years. I am beginning to suspect it is the latter.

Night 6: I talked to a friend who has been through this pain. Someone understands! I call my brother and cry with him a while. He has been through this too. This gives me hope and comfort in knowing that I am being understood. I make a promise to myself to call someone, anyone, before I get the urge to call Tonya again.

Dear Tonya,

I hate the fact that you are separate from me now. I hate the fact that you have someone else to hold you now. I hate the fact that you are hugging her, and not me. I hate the fact that I am feeling all this crap!

What are you doing? Are you flirting with her, courting her as you did me so long ago? Are you taking her to OUR favorite restaurants? Are you making love to her as I write this? Are you on your best behavior? Is she the girl of your dreams?

Just so your fragile, little ego doesn't get any bigger, rest assured that I do not want nor have I wanted you for a VERY long time. It has been so long since I have found you sexy, I don't even remember. No, you are NOT every dyke's dream. Far from it!

Michelle

Night 7: I knew the woman Tonya was with before me. Shirley and I were friends. Every time Tonya and I moved, we would have to discuss the "Shirley Box." The "Shirley Box" was the box containing all the memories of her former life with Shirley–the letters, the pictures, the mementoes. Tonya would ask me if she should throw it away. I convinced her not to. Although the past is over, it colors who we are today. Tonight I realized with shock that I have simply become another box in Tonya's life–the "Michelle Box." The "Michelle Box" will have the same destiny as the "Shirley Box." It will be put in the closet then moved to the garage, be sealed, be debated about whether it should be kept. Then it will be forgotten. I never thought that would be my destiny in her life.

Night 8: I can feel myself healing. With help, I have remembered what I had so blatantly forgotten. I was the one who made the decision to leave HER. She did not dump me for someone else, although that was the way it appeared for a while. I made the decision to leave her, and Tonya simply reacted the only way she knew how. But there is no escaping the pain her "reaction" has caused.

Healing the Wounds

Healing is my choice. I choose not to deny. At one of the most confusing, devastating times in my life–I choose to FEEL the pain.

The only way to be truly whole again is to have the courage to meet the pain and anguish head on, not to be enshrouded in new lovers, nor in futile attempts at reconciliation or in any other forms of denial. Those denial traps serve only one purpose–to cast an insidious veil over true feelings of loss, hurt and pain. They are enticing for a while because they work, because they make us forget.

Journal entry:

The night you fucked her I could not sleep. I knew. I decided to meditate and connect with my guiding Goddess. She took me to a new place that night. On the side of beautiful cliffs, there are natural hot springs. It is the middle of the night. The sky is piercingly clear and brilliant–the stars shine brightly. I immerse myself in the water. I feel fear, as if I don't know where the bottom is. The water black and murky encases me in its stream. I begin to float, letting my fear subside, remembering I am her child. I sit up and she begins to form herself from the stream. She floats above me. She knows I am fearful. I feel as if something deep and dark from under the water is going to grab my ankle and pull me under to a place I am terrified of. That "something" comes from the depths of depression. I do not want to go there again. I want to leave this place. My Goddess allows me to look through her eyes into the depths of my fear. Bright, clear light parts the water, exposing the beauty of shining crystals beneath. I see I have nothing to fear. Looking with her eyes there is only light. She illuminates the way; I just have to follow.

This gives me hope.

So, How Are You Getting Through This?

Depending on what day you ask, my reaction can range from: "Bite me, babe..." to "Sob, sob, whimper, sigh..." to "Oh, I don't know...I forget...I'm just doing it..." Seriously–and not so seriously–this is what I have been doing:

I cry, I cry, I cry and I cry. I meditate to connect with my guiding Goddess. I talk to my cat, Sweetz. (He threatened me if I didn't put his name in this.)

I concentrate on being in the present moment. I start each day with reading a meditation. I write in my journal about anything and everything. I only read books that empower me.

I reach out to friends–especially ones who have been through this type of pain. They are there to remind me I am loved and to give those much-needed hugs.

I am honest with my family as to what is going on. To my wonderful surprise, they are there to listen and to offer support. My brother has been an incredible anchor.

I accept no substitutions. From the color of my new trash-can to what I want for dinner, I see to it that I get *exactly* what I want. That's why I moved to the mountains; so that every morning I can look out my window and be in awe of the beauty that I now call home.

I yell "STOP" at the top of my lungs when I start to see those horrible pictures in my head, pictures of her loving THAT woman–and not loving me–even when I don't want to love HER anymore. (Does that make sense?) Anyway, my new neighbors probably think I'm crazy–but I do this to *retain* my sanity, not lose it.

I write nasty, lust-filled classified ads and fantasize about all the incredible, powerful, butch women who will be responding and wanting me. Be still, my beating heart!

I daydream about my ultimate fantasy woman and write a few choice stories about her. I hope she'll someday walk into my life and straight into my bed!

I walk around my home naked or in sexy lingerie–feeling every part of my womanly body, admiring it. I make love to myself as the urge takes me. Sometimes I watch in the mirror.

Since I am on the path of becoming a therapist, I joke that what I am going through now is required job training. When a future client comes to me with this type of pain–boy, will I be able to understand!

I am healing by writing my story. I can step back and honor the love I felt for Tonya, as well as the pain. And I can honor my courage to feel the loss.

Just One Last Word, I Promise

In the book *The Heart of Fire*, Fiona's teacher–her gran–tells her repeatedly that *every wound is an opening*. These wounds allow a chance for new blood to flow, to heal, and connect on a different plane of higher consciousness.

As lesbians, we experience our losses as even more consuming because we not only lose a woman we loved, but also part of ourselves on many levels. That woman represented an aspect of our biological mother. An aspect of the Goddess herself embodied in the woman we loved could have been lost. Maybe we need to look at all personal loss as an incredible gift of rebirth, and with that acceptance, find the courage to experience the pain that allows the joy of healing to occur.

Dear Tonya,

Is it time for goodbye? Is it time to wish you all the best in the world? I want to be able to say all those things, but as I write this now, I find I am not ready to do that. I do know, however, that that time is fast approaching.

I will thank you, though, for the one skill you so unselfishly taught me. It is something that will forever have a positive impact on my life–how to parallel park.

Michelle

P.S. I picked my first blackberry of the season today. I savored it; I did not share it. This simple act shows me I will survive all these feelings. In that moment, I have never been happier.

Release

Forget me not
(forget you now).

Foolish months
of lies to allude,

restless nights
in want
of you—

wishful ignorance
to forget the Other,

recall and recollection
to piece the past.

The four seasons
are no longer yours.

I do not want you.

Jessica Fair Stevens

Best of Friends...
'Til Death Do Us Part
by Charlie

I t was the spring of 1984 when I met Joanie. At the time I was in a relationship with a friend of hers who was abusive to her. When I got away two years later, I got a good job and moved into my own apartment. But one day I got home and all my things had been stolen; my furniture, plants and even my makeup. My boss gave me the money to get a restraining order against my ex, but first I spent three days lying on the floor...depressed. The next day, I went to work but my electricity was turned off by the time I returned home. That night, Joanie called. She told me my ex had done that. But she also asked if I was all right and if I'd like to have some company.

We talked by coil lamp until 3 a.m. I noticed I felt a small crush on her. Oh, I'd had similar feelings for Joanie before, but this time the feeling was stronger. I kept it to myself, not wanting to frighten her away.

Joanie and I spent a lot of time together. It had been two years since we'd met through my ex, and suddenly it was the two of us going to the movies, to the lake, dancing, playing.

One night I wanted to tell Joanie I loved her but was so afraid that I asked a friend to tell her for me. I took Joanie home and got the nerve to kiss her. At first, she acted silly and ran around my "bug," but the play soon stopped and we kissed. No fireworks, but nice. The next night, she invited me over to dinner. What a relief.

We got our own apartment the next month. I was deeply in love and I got a promotion at work to company director. Not bad for a 26 year old with no high school diploma. Life was good...until...Joanie's parents took her car away and she lost her job. I felt the stress of bills and my car problems. Then Joanie began drinking every day.

I considered getting out of the relationship, but we'd already had good times...and I was so in love. I felt I couldn't get enough of Joanie. As she slept, I would cuddle up to her and as she would breathe out, I would gasp her air in. She was all that mattered to me. I'd wanted her for so long and so much.

I'd gotten another raise and had bought furniture and other things to replace what had been stolen before. But the pressures I felt caused me to quit. I also hoped that Joanie might get her shit together and work with me if she saw how much we were in debt. Wrong! I was laying in bed when the electricity went off this time. Joanie and I somehow stayed together...but we lost the one apartment I ever felt was my home.

We moved in with someone we didn't really know, but we didn't have to pay rent because her mother owned the house. It would have been ideal, but I soon learned this person was a slob and the house was infested with cockroaches. It was so bad they crawled on us in bed, but we thought we had no choice. I began looking for a job right away, but I got extremely ill. The doctor said I could have died. I had no potassium in my body. In time, I got better and once again looked for a job as soon as I could get myself up and dressed. It was during this time that the things I'd bought for the other apartment were sold by the manager. Joanie and the women we lived with were supposed to move the things out. I'd paid $1300 for the sofa and only owed $300. The manager sold it for $50.

We lived in the cockroach infested house for six months. The night we moved into our new apartment, I cried, so relieved to be out of that house. We took a bubble bath and drank champagne. We were asleep on the floor when Joanie awakened me in the night. She was having a seizure. We figured it was caused by stress and too much champagne. We'd both been working and we were going to buy a sofa when Joanie got laid off. Again, finances forced us to move, this time with my boss. Life began settling down when the car broke down...again. I took out my frustration on Joanie, telling her to get a job or get out. We had a horrible fight. I should have known something was wrong because she knocked me down on the kitchen floor. I ran upstairs and locked the bedroom door. But Joanie kicked the door down. She had never laid a hand on me before.

When I woke up the next morning, Joanie wasn't in the apartment. I received a call from someone at a hospital. She had had a serious seizure. I was told at the hospital that I couldn't see her because I wasn't "family." But after her parents had the nerve to send her sister to ask me for $300.00, I said, "The hell with it," and walked to her room. All I wanted to do was hold Joanie close, but that didn't seem possible with her mother standing there. I held Joanie's hand and told her I was sorry.

The next day, surgery exposed a brain tumor. When I saw her on the gurney after the operation, I ran off yelling, "Fuck!" My mother took hold of me and we both cried. Joanie had brain cancer and the surgeon was unable to remove all of it.

I felt my life was over without Joanie and was sure her life would soon be over. It wasn't fair. Why her? Questions ran through my head.

I stayed drunk those days, didn't go to work, didn't give a damn about anything. One day I got so drunk at a bar that I knocked over an entire table of drinks. I just went crazy. Some friends took me home.

I wanted to die. I had gotten a gun from a friend, saying I needed it for protection. But that was a lie. So, while my friends sat in the living room, I walked upstairs, sat on the side of my bed, put the gun to my head and pulled the trigger. I still can see the fire from that gun.

I woke up in the hospital about three weeks later. My parents were there, crying. I hadn't realized how much they loved me until that day.

I was a mess. I couldn't move at all and I could barely talk. And I was angry. Angry that I wasn't dead. When you're shot in the head, you're supposed to die. But, no, not me. I was left on earth to suffer. I'd never realized how the brain controls everything.

No one told Joanie that I had shot myself because of her condition. My mother told me that Joanie was going to undergo chemotherapy and radiation, but that she was all right. She wanted me to "please hold on." So I started fighting for my life. When I called Joanie to tell her I was going away for a long time (for rehabilitation), she asked why I hadn't seen her recently. I told her the truth. She cried. I couldn't.

I had to relearn everything. I couldn't even hold my head up. But I had some good people working with me. They asked what I wanted to do more than anything. I said I wanted to dance again. I loved to dance. The doctors told my parents that if I lived, I'd be a "vegetable." I decided to prove them wrong.

I was inspired by a 60 year old woman who was a diabetic and had lost both her legs due to her illness. Before she arrived at Santa Barbara

Rehabilitation, I stayed very depressed. I'd been taken by ambulance from Bakersfield and the ride was painful. I didn't cry, though, because I'd done this to myself and felt I had no right to bitch to others.

I hurt from head to toe and couldn't stand to be touched anywhere. I was put into a large green wheelchair that supported my entire body.

Although the prognosis was so poor, I had promised my father I would get better for him. When I had regained consciousness in the hospital, it was Father's Day and I saw my father crying for the first time in my life. With this in mind, I was determined to walk again.

I had to learn how to sit up, as my body was limp. Then I learned to stand. Then to step. Then to walk. It wasn't easy, but both my parents are disabled and I knew they wouldn't be able to take care of me. Also, I'd worked in a rest home and there was no way I was going to allow myself to live in one of those.

On weekends, when the staff that worked with me was off, I'd lay in bed and exercise what parts of my body I could move. I'd have workers put me in a light wheelchair so I could try to get around on my own. I told my doctors that I was going to walk out of there, but although they knew I was determined, I think only Arlet, one of my therapists, believed I would.

Within six weeks I was walking a bit. Well, it was more like bouncing around. I waddled out of the rehabilitation clinic and back to my apartment. My bedroom was upstairs, so I'd sit on my butt and scoot up or down. We had a swimming pool, so every morning I'd get up, work my way to the pool, lay down, roll in and do my physical therapy. I sat in my wheelchair only one more time. I wasn't going to get back into that chair no matter what.

With Joanie having moved back with her parents, I lived with a male roommate. But problems began. Things were happening there with him and some "undesirables" that were there often. I didn't want to get involved with that, so after having lived on my own for eleven years, I moved back home with my dad and mom. I received Disability, so I saved my money for a car and got my driver's license back after a year. I also moved into my own place again.

It's been three years since I had to start my life over. I didn't realize I had this much strength. Oh, I get depressed, but those are the times I think of people in worse situations than my own, or back to when I couldn't get out of bed by myself. At times I get very lonely, but I don't allow life to get me down so far that I want to die. I go from day to day the best I can, with headaches, dizziness and feeling unbalanced all the time. But I figure I can lay in bed and complain or I can get up and get going.

Joanie and I are the best of friends, closer than we ever were the previous nine years. She lives with her parents, but we do just about everything together. People don't always know of our health problems because we force ourselves to get dressed and go out dancing. They don't believe we're just friends, but we don't care. We know how unfair life can be. We know how short it can be, too. We are best of friends 'til death do us part because she can die from her cancer any time and there is still one large chunk of bullet within my brain. If it moves...

My life and thinking have changed so much. Before I shot myself, I drank every day. A lot. I smoked three packs of cigarettes a day. Now my lungs are too weak to smoke. I don't do drugs, smoke or drink heavily anymore. Two glasses of wine are my limit. I don't need to walk into walls any more than I already do.

I cry from my loneliness sometimes, but I do write to a few pen pals, which helps. I fear telling any of them that I shot myself, though, because I don't think I'd ever hear from them again. I keep the hope that the saying that you only find love once in a lifetime isn't true. Without love, life is too lonely.

I fell out of love with Joanie. Too much had happened. At times, I wish I could fall back in love with her, but after three years, the only love I've felt for her is as my family.

Life is rough for everyone, but we've got to make the best of our time. I hate to see anyone feel pain, but that comes with life for a reason. We've got to hold our heads high no matter what happens.

I will never allow myself to fall for someone the way I did for Joanie. If I do care for someone again, I will keep up a wall. I gave up too much for her. I ended up losing a modeling career, commercials and being the director of a company. People must stay strong for themselves, learn to love and respect themselves. We can't put anyone before ourselves. No one is worth giving ourselves up for. Think about it. If the shoe were on the other foot, would someone else give up their life for you?

I dated a woman for nearly a year. We both spoke of living together someday, where we'd live, what kind of house it would be, and how we'd furnish it. We spent several nights a week at either her place or mine, but recently she said she doesn't think we should stay together. She couldn't give me any reasons, except that she doesn't know what she wants anymore. I'm in shock and crazed to think that our wonderful, or what I thought was wonderful, relationship is over. I can't think of anything else. Do you think she's just scared and will come back?

This is an emotional and painful time for you and it's important for you to focus on what you can and must do for yourself. You can't put your life on hold and wait and hope she'll come back. Waiting keeps you stuck in your pain and anger. When we wait, we aren't experiencing what we have to do to take care of ourselves in our own life this moment. We're almost stuck, placed on hold and not thinking about our own life and future plans. It's important to begin healing from this loss and accept that it's over. Be gentle with yourself, for if we were able to know the signs before the breakup, we would be more prepared.

Encore Presentation

The drama exists
    of perversity and persona—

the actors in which you intwine
    are most intriguing
    (or are they?)

Common fellows,
victims of foreplay...suitors of the Star.

The cast: questionable.

The heroine is only as good as her supporting cast.

                                        Jessica Fair Stevens

Heal or Perish
by Claire Connelly

I'm three months into healing from the loss of a four-year relationship with Cathy. It was quite a blow to me, because we had a holy union (I'm a minister) and had taken vows for life. I still don't know what the issues were because Cathy told me up until just before she left that she loved me and wouldn't leave me.

My only close friend, Joan, had broken up with her partner a few months ago. I invited Joan over frequently because I knew she was lonely, and she often stayed with Cathy when I went out at night to classes or meetings. I thought it was great they had one another for company.

But three months ago I came home from work and Cathy told me she was in love with Joan and that they had decided to live together. Cathy moved out that night, refusing to discuss anything with me. I was plunged into chaos. My spouse and my best friend! I am in my mid-fifties and have no family on the West Coast, where I have lived for five years. Whom to turn to? I work as a volunteer counselor, and I knew I was in crisis and into a suicidal depression. I called a therapist and set up weekly appointments.

We set up priorities. Finances were my major concern-Cathy and I had merged assets, rented a large home, taken out an auto loan, and charged thousands of dollars to my credit cards. With Cathy gone, the household income was cut in half; I was left with a home I couldn't keep up and bills I couldn't pay. To try to solve this, I drew up a contract with Cathy for monthly payments against joint bills and advertised for a roommate to share expenses.

I couldn't sleep, I couldn't eat, and I couldn't stop crying. I had my family doctor prescribe a tricyclic antidepressant to help me sleep at least for brief periods, forced myself to eat three small meals daily, and played spiritual music and hymns several hours each day. I reread a little book called *How to Survive the Loss of a Love*. I tried to keep my daily life as routine as possible and kept myself busy running errands, mowing the lawn, cleaning the house, and increasing my hours of volunteer work.

The worst feelings to deal with were that I was unlovable and faulty in some way. For one thing, I am 14 years older than Cathy. Was she running away from my aging? Another problem is that I am disabled from paid work because of osteoarthritis and am living on a fixed income. Am I decrepit and destined for poverty? How could the two people I loved most in the world do this to me unless I was a terrible person? Rejection seems to make us feel that somehow we deserve it.

I took a two week trip back to the East Coast and commiserated with relatives and friends. I had told them years ago about my homosexuality, so it wasn't a problem, and I got support there. But eventually I had to return to my life and to a now-empty house where Cathy and I had lived together in so much love and bliss–at least that is the way I perceived it.

After about four weeks, I found I could sleep again, although Cathy and Joan haunted my dreams. And my appetite returned. Within six weeks, I found myself laughing again and singing at home. Generally, I tend to be a joyful person. The best thing was that I didn't revert to old patterns of wallowing in self-pity and drinking myself into a stupor. I had overcome more than thirty years of alcoholism just before I met Cathy, and this breakup was the first real test of my sobriety.

While I cry from time to time and fear the long, lonely nights, some hope has returned. I see an attractive woman and wonder if we could be friends. I make a mental list of all the things about Cathy that bothered me and am grateful that I don't have to deal with them anymore. I wonder what negative karma the new lovers will have to work out as a result of betraying and hurting me.

Since the lesbian social groups in my community are limited, I can't help running into Cathy and Joan. The breakup is still fresh, and the atmosphere is strained when we collide in public–although we are civil to one another. I have the added burden of being a community activist, living in a fishbowl. And now I am the topic of gossip. No longer a respected role model in a stable, monogamous relationship, now I am just another gay woman who has been jilted by her lover and mocked by her "best friend." I know I'll live it down. But when?

As a counselor, I know that grief is a process and that there is no way around it; one has to go through it. I grieve the loss of my loved one and am astonished that I misjudged Joan–she was never a friend, only a predator. I know I must forgive them both in order to free myself of them. My love for Cathy is so great that it transcends anger and vengeance. I wish her happiness. And Joan was lonely and desperate, but still I can't forgive her. Not yet.

I know that it is a lesbian convention to become friends with old lovers and their new significant others. Yet I cannot see at this point how I could ever feel comfortable with them as a couple. I have been wounded too deeply, my life has been severely disrupted, and my leadership in the community has been compromised.

But with every day that passes, I heal a little more. Maybe someday I will be able to trust in friendship again. Who knows, I might even love again and be loved in return. Who knows?

Still Looking for Juliet
by Romeo

Anita:

I heard that you were looking for breakup stories and how women healed from their losses. I say with pain that I'm still in the process and I am hoping this letter will help. I guess I should give a little history.

I met...well, I will call her Ms. Big Butt for the purpose of this letter. (I love BBW). I was dazzled by her icy blue eyes, short brown hair, and tall voluptuous figure. After talking to her for awhile, her Southern charm showed through.

Our relationship was based on friendship. We talked for hours. We'd built a trust by which we could always talk and work things out. She was my Juliet.

We'd been seeing each other four months when a neighbor complained to the landlord and gave Big Butt a hard time about my being there. So we moved in together.

We got two kittens, hers and hers (which I took care of). After we moved, though, the communication began to crumble quickly. We both withdrew. I had feelings of panic and terror that I didn't understand then. All I knew was that something was wrong. I now know that I was beginning to have body memories of abuse long forgotten.

The fights got worse as the memories got stronger. Everything was my fault. It was my stuff to deal with, I was told. But Big Butt decided she needed some space, so she went back home (where the buffalo roam).

During the four weeks she was gone, Slimer, Big Butt's ex-girlfriend, showed up at the door and told me Big Butt said it was okay for her to move in. Slimer then proceeded to do everything she could to undermine my relationship with Big Butt. She'd tell me that she'd gotten a letter from Big Butt and ask if I wanted to hear it. When I confronted Big Butt, I discovered that she had written the letters long before I was in the picture. Things were tense.

One night I arrived home to the sight of Slimer and Big Butt on the couch. Big Butt announced that the memories (of abuse) and the neediness were my stuff to deal with and said one of us (meaning me) was moving out!

What happened to "we're in this together?" I was devastated. I had lost Juliet.

I didn't believe much in that counseling thing, but I was in such desperate pain that I just wanted it to stop. I called several counselors and talked to them about their philosophy and practices. I made an appointment with the one that gave the answers I liked best. She asked for a verbal agreement that I would not kill myself and that if I got in that state of mind again, I would call for help. I agreed, knowing full well that I didn't mean it.

I tried to be friends with Ms. Big Butt, but the chemistry was too strong. Once I asked her if I could get something from the apartment that I'd forgotten. When I got there, I asked her where Cyrano (not his real name) was. He was our/my four-month-old kitten. Big Butt said that "he's around here somewhere." I found Cyrano in the basement, curled in a ball, shivering and looking up at me with his big ten cent eyes and long nose. I picked him up and told Big Butt that I was taking him with me. She told me that if I'd take him, she didn't want him back.

I got a letter saying that Big Butt didn't want me to contact her in any way because it was too painful. Months passed when I ran into her at the Gay Pride festival. I was standing with one of my closest friends of several years (we'll call her Howdy Doodoo) when Ms. Big Butt walked over and spoke to Howdy. She didn't even look at me.

I had so many unanswered questions. I later called, begging her for answers so I could get some peace of mind. Big Butt's response was, "Well, I have a girlfriend, if that helps." (That sentence still rings in my head.)

I felt the knife plunge into my stomach while darkness flooded my body and tears filled my eyes. It truly was over. I called Howdy Doodoo, looking for some comfort. She told me that she had known for quite awhile. She proceeded to tell me that she and Big Butt and Big Butt's new girlfriend had done this and done that and how she had a wonderful time. *I had learned the true meaning of betrayal.*

I began writing: poems, short stories, letters (that I didn't send), filled with the feelings that were running through me. I allowed myself to feel them, but when they got too strong, I'd stop and do something to take my mind off them. I'd go to a park that isn't very far from my house. It has a basketball court, swings, and a slide. I made good use of them.

I discovered that weightlifting is a great way for me to release anger. I used it to help me focus my anger, get it out, and go on with my life.

I began drawing again. It had been a long time. I got out all my art supplies and laid them on the floor. I kept going back to a big red marker. I graduated to black and white drawings. If things got too painful, I'd try to turn it into a cartoon.

I found that humor helps take the power out of the pain and makes it a little more bearable. I'm happy to say that I use all 48 colors (Crayola) now.

I owe the most gratitude to Cyrano. He's not so little now. When I thought I couldn't take it anymore, all I had to do is look at him and it was as if he knew. He'd come to me and sit on my drawing or writing paper and just purr. Knowing that someone still loved me was enough for me to go on.

Every so often, I run into Big Butt, her girlfriend, and Howdy Doodoo. They look right through me. It weighs on my heart knowing that two people I cared about are not in my life anymore. But I am grateful to have discovered that living well has been the best revenge.

My last relationship ended when my lover and my best friend had an affair. I've heard of this happening to others. Is this more prevalent in the Lesbian community? I've lost my lover and best friend. How can I ever trust again after this betrayal?

This is common and prevalent in the Lesbian community. Friendships are our greatest source of support in our lives and in our Lesbian experience. The trust you had between your lover and best friend is damaged. It will be difficult to repair and never feel betrayed, suspicious, or distrustful of them again. You placed your trust in your best friend and your lover and expected each one to be respectful. Each person was like a family member. Your friend was perhaps like a sister.

It's important to work through your feelings over both your lover and friend. This means getting in touch with the anger and hurt which can be frightening when you think of how much you cared about both those people. You might experience the breakup with the friend in the same manner you do with your lover. It's important to rebuild new social relationships and to be loving and kind toward yourself in all ways.

Single Bed Pantoum

I see the twin bed in there
all crisp with new flowered sheets
so cozy in the corner of the room
waiting to be slept in

All crisp with new flowered sheets
the colors mauve, blue, serene
waiting to be slept in
a space just big enough for me

The colors mauve, blue, serene
calming me down after this long day
a space just big enough for me
I wonder if it could fit two?

Calming me down after this long day
moving boxes up and moving boxes down
I wonder if it could fit two?
I wonder, could there be such a lover?

Moving boxes up and moving boxes down
growing sweaty and hot and tired
I wonder, could there be such a lover
to make love in a twin bed with me?

Growing sweaty and hot and tired
spending her passion and mine
to make love in a twin bed with me
again and again, all night long.

Spending her passion and mine
Giving hot kisses, saying "I don't care"
again and again all night long
the colors mauve, blue and serene.

Giving hot kisses, saying "I don't care"
a woman with soft passionate mouth
the colors mauve, blue and serene
hour after hour after hour.

A woman with soft passionate mouth
a woman with eyes flecked with fire
hour after hour after hour
until we are spent and sleep.

A woman with eyes flecked with fire
waiting, wanting to be slept with
until we are spent and sleep
so cozy in the corner of the room.

Waiting, wanting to be slept with
(this woman, this woman is me)
so cozy in the corner of the room
in a space just big enough for me.

This woman, this woman is me
I am called to be my own lover
in a space just big enough for me
waiting to be slept in.

                              Susan J. Friedman

So J'm Leaving She Said
by Cathy Chambers

I'd expected it. I think that on some level I knew...was just waiting for it to happen. Yet it was something that I did not expect, could not expect. I had not known how loss would be like a punch, like fists again and again hitting the gut.

She told me on my thirtieth birthday that she was in love with another woman, a fellow actor. And at first I was relieved to have it at last in words. It had not been easy living with her as she was falling in love, watching but not knowing exactly what was happening. I was shaken when she told me–for I felt especially vulnerable turning 30–but it did not seem to me that it would be the end of our relationship.

Three months later, she decided that it would be. She was too heart-sickly in love to be able to accommodate herself any longer to our relationship, which had become like a third person in our dealings with each other. I did not let go quickly or easily. It was important to me to stay in that relationship in a way it perhaps should not be to anyone. I no longer recognized myself outside of it. I was not sure who I was without her beside me, inside me, part of me.

A few weeks ago, while sorting through a long-untouched pile of papers, I came across the journal that I'd kept during the first months of our breakup. It was both familiar and completely foreign to me. Reading, I remembered, sometimes vividly, the specifics of that survival. I remembered taking long walks down to the beach where I'd sit and read or write between the shadows of palm trees. "Better to have loved and lost than never to have loved at all," I would repeat to myself, the rhythm of the words matching the pace of my walking and keeping my mind from thought, keeping the tears from my eyes. But I hadn't remembered that I'd written so little about the breakup itself. The concentration of images, dreams, daydreams seems strange now but perhaps I wrote knowing that analysis, so often self-defeating, was not the way to heal. I wrapped my wounds in organic imagery and waited for time and a regeneration.

My legs are amazing–not long, as I've always wanted them to be, but muscular in a slim way now from bike riding. There are bulges in my thighs that flex when I walk, flex attractively, not without strength. My hips are less padded, my stomach is flat, my ribs are wide and thin; they fly up wing-like when I take a deep breath. I could be lifted with a gust of wind under them, filling them. Instead there is only my heart, lonely and puny. But my arms are molded; they curve in and out of muscle and bone and my hands are free to feel the air, to make shadows on the sidewalk in front of me.

I practice seeing myself as someone who will again be loved.

I thought, "I must save myself," and closed my eyes. Patterned against the lids were images of flowers, images in dark batiked colors–dark red, dark green. "And so I shall save myself so." I imagined my head a flower, petals blooming from my brain.

This pain should be good for something. It should open me up to myself with surgical precision, a clean cut. A drop of blood wells at severed connection but is clamped off.

I want to see a scar.

I want this pain to turn me around, shake me up, thrown me down hard. I want to be left mind dazed, knowing viscerally what is important.

I want to be able to put myself back together.

Trees impassive, massive strength, rooted to the center, centered life. Branches expose to the world the life in light. Risking branches in winter, naked when there seems no hope in spring but trusting with ancient patience that the sap will run again.

In transition, transient. Caravans, pulling up stakes, moving out, unwashed behind the ears. Let these ties that bind, snap and break; let them rust forgotten underfoot, these chains of the heart. For there can be now only a new freedom, only a way out.

Blood, elemental, seeping from me in slow pulsation. Some months I am sapped by its loss, energy gone with it out of me, but not today. Now, here in the sun, I feel as if from some past culture, avowedly powerful with this red flow, this bright red flowering, this ability to bleed without losing vitality. My sense of life is intense.

I want to lie back with red blossoms in my hair. That most of all. I want there to be water and waves and light. I want to stand with roots, to wave with winds of change. I believe in this. Forget the details; they will work themselves out in magic that I create. The moon is full tonight. All spells are possible.

March will be over in a few hours. I would like to stay up until midnight and bury finally, with carousing and good cheer, the closing moments of this month.

Dozing, my brain is, I think, in its sunburned body. Parts inside ache; my teeth, the nerves that go to and from my ears and something alongside my hipbone that I imagine to be my appendix. I feel I'm floating on waters of illness and yet am not ill, have no fever, no nausea, nothing to treat.

For years I tried to train myself to a life alone, to accept loneliness with stoic asceticism. That was before I met you. While living with you, loving you, I thought more optimistically. You were there, not always when I needed, but usually close, and it's funny how viscerally I expect you still; the outside door opens and in my gut, before my brain says "no," I know it's you coming home.

Last night I lay awake as I often do, not crying, but thinking things out. The moon was waxing. I lay in bed wondering about needs, desires, possession, power, strength, autonomy...words like mantras, chanted spells.

I thought about life alone again.

Dreams buzzed like hornets, angry dreams buzzing in my head with a fury I haven't expressed awake. Dreams in which I yelled, spit out the venom that has been collecting in secret sacs these months and when I woke, before I realized I'd been asleep and dreaming, I expected anger and fighting. Then I realized that none of it had happened, that no one had actually witnessed my Medusa-like rage, and I was relieved and fell asleep again.

This morning seems bright with promise; I am giddy with expectation, free of the substance that gnarled my grip.

I don't stand within a therapeutic framework and "recovery" is not a word I use comfortably. But years have passed; time heals. I certainly do not feel and have not felt for a long time that constant sense of loss, of gaping aches. With new friends, a new academic direction, a new and sometimes wonderfully surprising partner, I am not only learning to recognize myself outside of that first relationship, but am also moving beyond the breakup, can get past the image of myself as an "ex," as the one she left.

Still, however, I am sometimes angry when I see her, sometimes hurt. I would like to cry, but don't. I am forced to realize that even with the intervening years I'm not completely "recovered" and wonder if I ever will be.

Sometimes when we get together and talk, even if only for a few minutes, our words grow into meaning, become more than flat objects that merely skim the surface. Not always, but often enough. We tap the source of a common genesis. And when I leave, I feel something deep inside me, in my stomach or in my soul, stirs and briefly flops awake and I am happy and I am sad, at the same time.

I've been wading. My feet are sandy; the ragged edges of my shorts are wet and cold against my legs. March is not yet summer but the day as soon as I woke seemed to need something in it besides the usual coffee and Sunday paper. I wanted to be somewhere else, to go someplace by myself. My depression from yesterday hung on and made me restless, a depression of gaping aches that is dangerous when I'm tired. The morning needed to be recreated and separated from the day before. Fog over the ocean promised solitude. I went wading.

Standing at the edge of wave, I turned back to the shore and could see my footprints in the wet sand. I thought, "This is me. Here I am. Let go. There is nothing more."

Upon publication

    within the threshold of Death
    of the Heart...

The mocking nature of Reality (awaits).

J say,

where is the paper
and the pen to write?

Jessica Fair Stevens

The Heart of the Matter
by Anita L. Pace

Dear Danielle,

It's been two years since you said you didn't want a committed relationship with me, and nearly as long since you moved away. There's still so much I don't understand that I've been trying to. I don't know how our relationship began so warm, loving, and fun, yet is without even a friendship now. That's why I'm writing.

Remember the night we met in that support group? Everyone was talking about the "toys" at the Pleasure Chest. I spoke about that place to a woman on my right. You sat on my left. I kept rehearsing in my mind how to ask if you were going out to eat after the group ended. But I was so nervous. I turned to you and mistakenly asked, "Are you going to the Pleasure Chest?" You laughed, but I was extremely embarrassed.

At the French Market, you sat next to me. You only had orange juice because you were going to have surgery the next morning. I didn't know whether or not to ask what your surgery was for, but I wanted you to know I was interested in you.

I thought of calling you the next day, but I didn't want to seem overly interested. That's, of course, because I was. When you called me a few days later, it took me three hours just to tell you I'd invite you along to see *Field of Dreams* with my friends if I wasn't so scared. I was about to hang up when you said, "Wait, what theater are you going to?"

I acted completely engrossed in the movie, but I kept wondering what was going to become of us the entire time. I didn't know how to say goodbye to you later as we stood by your car. You told me you were planning to leave Los Angeles when you finished school. I was disappointed. But I wasn't about to tell you, "Dammit! I thought we might live happily ever after." That would've been just a bit presumtuous after having spent but a few hours together. (We thought it amusing when you later told me you wished you hadn't told me you were planning on leaving the city.)

You came into my life when I was starting to feel like a human again after Tina left six months earlier. I'd since met someone I liked, but she liked me only as a friend. I can't forget the night I had a date with you but broke it to be with her because she was depressed. I wanted to be there for her, but I was also afraid of you.

That feeling soon ended, you know. When I went to your place for the first time two days later, my stomach hurt a lot. Nerves. I'd intended to tell you I wasn't sure what I wanted. But when I saw you sitting at your drafting table, wearing walking shorts and concentrating on your work, a spark ignited. You'd seemed so interested in me at first that I got scared. But when I saw you engrossed in your creativity, my attraction for you multiplied. Do you recall how you shook when you hugged me goodbye outside your parents' house?

Dani, it was a special night when you missed your class and spent it with me. We hadn't planned it. It was romantic, warm, loving.

I was relieved that I didn't freak out when you had to leave. I felt secure and figured I'd finally learned how to be involved with someone without being enmeshed. I was convinced you were the love of my life.

Do you remember when you gave me that swimming lesson? I have such a fear of water, but you got me floating on my back. I felt so much joy that I was laughing inside. I saw the look of pride on your face and couldn't hold back the excitement. Of course, I sank as soon as I began laughing.

Remember that night we listened to that Dionne Warwick record? You seemed so elated that I liked her. You gave me the impression that that commonality made you think that I was the one for you. Or was it that I was an aspiring writer? You did say you wanted to be involved with a writer.

I was pretty damn scared of meeting your parents. Wasn't it something that your mother made us dinner and put us alone in the dining room. We kept saying, "Do you think they know? Do you think this is their way of letting us know?"

Your mother seemed to like me more. She even gave you a hundred dollars when we went to Disneyland. God, she told us to spend the night in a motel near there. I wonder how much fun you'd ever have without the urging of your mother. We had a great time at Disneyland, but you sure got irritable as I drove home. I started seeing your changeable moods more and more.

Your schoolwork was grueling. But I loved helping you with your projects when I could. I was in awe of your talent, perhaps more so since I can't even draw a good stick figure. I learned a lot from you. You told me how you look around at everything when you need answers for your projects. I notice that I often do the same thing myself now.

Since you didn't have another chair in your room I always sat on the floor. I felt touched when you turned to me once and said, "If I was working and we had our own place, you wouldn't have to sit on the floor." Every so often you'd drop a statement like that. I'd feel loved and wanted.

The word "love" was more difficult for you than for me. I think you said the three sentences that scared you most are "I love you," "I miss you," and "I need you." I thought it sad, and also know that I often wanted to say all three sentences to you. Sometimes you sang along with Gloria Estefan: "I don't want to lose you now." I took it personally.

Remember when we looked at kitchenware at Target when we passed the jewelry department? I was so surprised when you intimated that you wanted a ring. I definitely had wanted to give you one, but I thought it would scare the wits out of you. And so I bought you a simple gold band. I felt happy to see you wear it, to know you wanted it.

And you were upset that you didn't have the money to buy me a ring also. But you didn't let that stop you. You made a ring of wire with string wrapped around it. It would be my temporary ring, you said.

We spoke of the future, of living together, of having the house and the dog that would join my geriatric cat. But the answer to living in Los Angeles *vs.* moving to a city that would best suit your career was repeatedly changed. I kept telling you, "We'll deal with that when we get there." I believed that what mattered was our love and that we would cope with whatever happened.

Taking a trip during your school break was exciting. It started off great when I turned from getting something out of the closet to see a small box. Inside was that beautiful gold band. Just when I was questioning if your feelings were mellowing toward me, you gave me that ring. I felt loved.

But the trip was a continuation of what was becoming a pattern: closeness, distance, closeness, distance. I recall feeling most loved during that time when you put calamine lotion on my nearly 60 mosquito bites I got while we hiked. (You didn't even get one.)

I knew you were scared of commitment. And I was petrified of being left by you. I began to grab, knowing full well you'd react like a bobbing apple eluding a person's grasp.

I thought what we needed was to spend more time with others. I preferred that we do things with couples. So I thought it was good when we went out with Cherry and saw Sex, Lies and Videotape. And I thought it was romantic of me to drive up Mulholland Drive afterwards. I don't believe I'd ever done that before with someone.

I don't know how it came up, but telling me you still were emotionally involved with your ex hit me with the force of a bulldozer. I never expected it. I guess that news was my own Pearl Harbor, a surprise attack, so to speak. I hurt so badly that the thought of driving over the cliff crossed my mind. I was so in love with you. I'd thought your inconsistency with me had to do with your fear of intimacy. I didn't think another person was involved. You said you were confused. You said you loved me. That's all I needed to hang in there. I couldn't bear the thought of the alternative.

I tried to be a supportive partner/mate/friend through your turmoil. But I attempted to calm mine by finding ways to bring you closer to me. I made the outcome of our relationship the basis on whether I would be alright or not. I couldn't imagine life without you. But I loved you and wanted to help you through your fear.

However, you then started telling me that you weren't sure I was the "right" one. You'd had a good relationship (by your assessment) and compared me to her. I became depressed, irritable, and anxious. My happiness turned to a feeling of being on guard all the time. It was difficult for me to be open when you were.

I'd been in therapy for some time when I met you, and shortly after, I told my therapist we could deal with my anxieties and phobias instead of relationships because I didn't have any problems in my new relationship with you. It's no wonder I'm superstitious about saying everything is okay. I managed to have one week where I didn't need to speak about my feelings and concerns regarding a relationship. I was petrified of being abandoned by you.

I began art therapy to help me get out of my head and into my feelings. I needed the talk therapy, but I needed to find another avenue to myself. My drawings were clear, even if I can't draw. I was hurt, angry, and scared. And I feared you'd get frustrated if you knew exactly how I felt. In retrospect, you probably did anyway.

It seemed the relationship was on the upswing on that awful night in 1989. You had bronchitis, but still you called me to join you to shop for a project. When we got to your home, your father did not appreciate my concern for you and he wanted you to stay home that night. I remember how you ached hearing that. You went to my place, but when your mother called and you spoke privately, you got more withdrawn. I can't blame all our problems on your father, but I know it didn't help that he wasn't crazy about me visiting almost every evening. And, although you didn't tell me, I think I could assume he didn't approve of me or of us. You drifted further and further from me and I felt lost. I'd helped you get into therapy, but I felt that, despite your pain, you had far more control over your life than I did at that time.

I'd been writing in my journal every day. Putting my feelings and the day's events on paper helped me keep some sanity. Maybe I should have been spending a lot more time with others, but I was afraid you'd use that to think I was abandoning you. I didn't want to play games. I didn't want to try to make you feel insecure just so you might come running after me. Despite everything that was happening, I believed you loved me. I also knew your work at school was not a picnic. You

were committed to doing exceptionally well there. I know you feared ending up at McDonald's at times.

But I didn't give myself as much compassion and understanding as I gave you. I felt increasingly inadequate. I had no career. I believed I had no special talent. I questioned why you would want to be with me. I'd felt secure and adequate when I had your love. But it changed. You'd been the one who pursued me in the beginning. I ended up chasing you.

Our relationship was undefined. Sometimes you thought you were becoming increasingly committed. Other times you said you didn't know what you wanted. I wanted to be with you. I wanted to share my life with you. I wanted to create with you. I wanted to live with you. I wanted to travel with you. I wanted to feel free to tell you I loved you. But you didn't seem to want to hear those things.

I thought I was no longer seeing you at your parents' house because of your father. I'd thought you came over less because of your studies. But I didn't know what the truth was. I still don't.

I was so depressed. I worked with incredible emotional pain. I felt so alientated and lost. I was suspicious that you were seeing your ex, but you said you were busy with school. I didn't always believe you, which only upset you. You wanted me to trust you. I wanted to trust you. But then I doubted you loved me anymore.

I'd gone to the *Course in Miracles* lectures before I met you, but had sloughed off when I was with you. I went back. I spoke to others of my pain. I searched for answers and tried to detach. Yet I felt I was in quicksand and the quicksand was my attachment to you. Remember the night I showed up unexpectedly? You'd slit your finger with an

exacto knife accidentally and were pretty scared about it. You seemed relieved that I showed up and took you to the hospital. But when I tried to kiss you, you turned your head away. I would've paid to know what was going on.

And then you graduated. I thought we'd spend more time together then. You'd thought you'd be ready to commit by then. But no. You said you weren't ready for a relationship with anyone. I'd waited so long for us to really be together and then you said you couldn't.

The next month seemed better. We took a trip to Nevada and gambled a little in Laughlin. But when we returned, you got withdrawn again. I felt horrible when, around this time, we went out and had a good time only to return to your house with your ex visiting your parents. They obviously liked her. I felt out of place.

You took a liking to the song *I'm Not in Love*, and I kidded you about it. But I feared the title was the truth for you. The mixed messages continued.

I'd told you I wouldn't move out of Los Angeles with you unless you could make a commitment. When you got your job in Oregon, I was very happy about it. That's when I knew how much I loved you. I knew how much you wanted that job. It was great helping you with the move, driving up together. Living with you for three weeks was bittersweet. I loved being with you, but I knew I'd have to leave. You seemed relieved when I told you I would stay one day beyond what I'd planned. But sometimes, I felt you didn't want me there.

Why did you cry when you read the letter of love before I left? Was it because you knew you didn't love me? Was it because you did, but didn't want to?

I was miserable back in Los Angeles. I missed you constantly. I started group therapy for lesbians going through a breakup. That helped. Hearing the stories of others put my situation in perspective and I didn't feel as alone.

I kept writing in my journal. All my feelings and the day's events were recorded. And when you called to say that maybe our relationship could be repaired, I was elated. But you also had bronchitis. "I remember how good you were to me when I was sick," you said. I told you we should see if you feel the same way about repairing our relationship when you're well.

I didn't hear from you for quite awhile after that, and when you did call, it was a mess. I know I laid out all my feelings. I know you hated it. I just couldn't hold it in any longer. Even if I'd said it all before, it wanted to come out again. Seven hours of ugly conversation. We both felt awful. You cried and asked if I was happy that I'd broken you down. I wasn't trying to. I was broken down.

You said you felt like never talking to me again. You've pretty much kept to that, Dani. After that conversation from hell, I became deeply depressed. I went to codependent's anonymous meetings. I figured I must be codependent since I was in so much pain over you. I started writing stories that I hoped to put in a book someday, but I really had to push myself. I went to as many social gatherings as I could find in *Lesbian News* (Los Angeles-based newspaper).

I'd gone to groups at *Connexus* in Los Angeles. But when it had to close its doors, I worked on getting a single's group started. One group did begin, but it lasted only a short while.

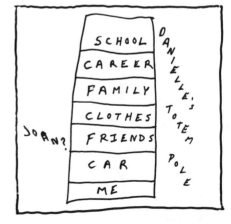

I needed to be around women that I could talk to, women who I could have fun with, but could also be honest with about my pain. I'd pretty much given up on hearing from you.

But then I remembered your birthday was coming up. I thought how you might be lonely. I wanted to be there with you and asked if you'd like me to come. You did. I planned for weeks to see you. I had a countdown on my calendar. Living with the idea of seeing you soon helped me through the lonely days.

I was damned depressed again when you said you'd be coming to Los Angeles around your birthday so you could attend a reunion of your schoolmates. You didn't think it made sense for me to drive up when you were coming down.

My depression lessened when you said that you could perhaps spend the night at my place after your sister picked you up at the airport. And then we'd go to the *Course in Miracles* lecture together. But you never called. You never showed up. Thank God my friend, Khris, was there for me.

In my desperation, I went to a psychic. He told me that we'd be together someday. Hearing that soothed me. The hope of this happening helped me hang on.

This psychic told me that I must see you when you come to Los Angeles, if only for a few minutes, or I would never see you again.

You'd been in Los Angeles for over a day and were about to return on Sunday afternoon. Dropping my pride, I called you. When your phone was busy for several minutes, I raced to your parents' house. You

didn't look happy to see me. Had your feelings completely died already?

You were about to leave for brunch before leaving for the airport. "I'd be glad to drive you to the airport," I said. You didn't think it was a good idea. Your eyes had a cold look. Did I know you anymore? Did I ever?

I'm not sure how I found out your ex was invited to the brunch with your family. That made me feel real good, Dani. Real good.

It seemed you left open the possibility that I'd be able to drive you to the airport, but later you called and said there just wasn't enough time. The truth was that seeing me wasn't on your agenda. As much as it would have hurt, it would have been better had I known from the start that you didn't love or possibly even like me anymore.

And I don't know why. Wasn't I the same person you said you could tell things to that you couldn't tell to others? Wasn't I the one who listened and stayed with you when you said that some of your statements had frightened others off?

I'm not saying I was wonderful. But I loved you. I listened to you. I worked on trusting you even when my insides were saying not to. I told you I shouldn't try to stop you from seeing your ex because that would only make you want to see her more.

When you left, my depression worsened again. I searched for more therapy. I went to a psychiatric hospital where the nurse wanted me to check in as an inpatient. I settled for being an outpatient, going to various groups from 10 a.m. until late afternoon every day. I was with others who were depressed, had multiple personalities, were coming off drugs, and every other psychiatric problem. The interaction helped. Having to be somewhere at a certain time helped.

With so much difficulty sleeping at night, I began playing Nintendo. I got a baseball game in which I could create teams and name the players. I was angry at you, Dani. So I named a team "Danielle's Deceivers" and named all the players "Danielle." Then I got out my anger by throwing the video ball at your head or striking you out. It was a safe way to deal with the anger.

I'd been determined not to call you, but after several months of limited relief, I decided to contact you. You talked to me, even if not a whole hell of a lot. You let me know you were in a relationship and living with someone. Whoa! After you had told me it would be a long time before you'd be ready for a relationship, the "long time" must have sped by. I didn't act devistated, but I was. You told me you had a new life, new friends. Wow. I got the feeling I'd just been someone until a better someone came around. Was I, Dani?

You said you should've never gotten involved with me. You said you'd lowered your standards. What did you mean by that?! Did you forget how you had said several times that you trusted me more than anyone? Did you forget how you cried on my shoulder because you were overwhelmed by the feelings of loving and being loved?

The sentences that glued to my memory bank were, "Don't call me or write to me. I'll call you when I need to." I've long since calmed down, but what the hell did you mean by that? Were only your needs important? Was everything to be on your terms? Did we never have a two-way friendship? I despised you for quite awhile after hearing that.

But I guess that was good, because the anger helped me get on with my life. I stopped group therapy and looked at how to take charge of my life without it having anything to do with you.

I decided to move out of Los Angeles. I'd considered it for several years, but had been afraid. I'd grown stagnant there and wanted a major challenge as moving would be. I wanted to meet a new set of people and live where there is clean air and more open space. I wanted to meet new women and potential partners.

Yes, Dani, I moved to the same city where you live. I wanted a city with a mixed political climate as Portland has. I wanted a better health environment. I wanted a city with a large lesbian population. But I didn't want you anymore.

Moving was part of my healing. It made me think of other things. I was scared, Dani. Petrified. I awakened hyperventilating many nights before the move. But I had to shake myself of us. I did not want to live and die in Los Angeles. Approaching 40, I saw my mortality and didn't like the obituary I foresaw.

I decided to write a book about the pain of lesbian breakups. Then I decided an anthology would be best. So in May, 1990, I started the process of creating such a book. It wasn't easy, but that was okay. I received stories for the book with accompanying letters from lesbians so glad I was doing it. They were supportive and I delighted in speaking to many of them on the phone and writing to all of them. I know you understand that satisfaction because I've seen you experience that with your own projects.

Remember when you had to create a project for the homeless? We went to Skid Row in Los Angeles and saw the cardboard homes of some. And for weeks you worked on creating a Christmas meal package. It was terrific, Dani. I was so proud of what you'd created. I was inspired by your ability to concentrate. Sometimes I see items in stores. I think of how you could design it better.

A few months ago, after living in Portland for several months, I saw you in that record store. So many times I had thought I might run into you somewhere. When I turned and saw you, my heart raced. I hoped you'd look at me. Why didn't you? Did I do anything so terrible that you have had to close up to me entirely?

Two years have passed since I ached over you, slept five hours a night and lost 15 pounds. But, Dani, I still think about you. Everything I've done to help myself was valuable. My friends and my actions kept me alive. Had I not been afraid of death, I might have taken my life. I know you aren't a cold person. I know you feel a lot more than you want to. There was warmth and love between us. I wish you hadn't felt it necessary to throw it all away.

I'm in a new relationship now. She knows how I think of you. She knows I loved you like I've loved few others. And she treats me like few have ever treated me. I need to remember that when I miss you. She's honest with me, she gives to me, she wants to share everything with me. And, even though it's painful for her, she's putting me before her parents who would like to break us up. I need those things from a partner.

I think I will heal from our breakup when it no longer matters to me to know why you won't speak to me, why you pulled away from me, why it was so hard for you to say "I love you," why you were dishonest with me.

Until then, I'll keep hoping we can talk again someday. Either way, I've learned to never trust anyone completely. I've learned to not put anyone above me. I've learned that not arguing doesn't mean a good relationship. I've learned that life doesn't always make sense, and neither do the people we love.

You meant a lot to me, maybe too much for your comfort. I'm learning to mean a lot to me, Dani. It's too uncomfortable when I don't.

I hope you are well.

Love, Anita

Four Years
by Jean Allen

Four years ago I was chained to a hospital gurney to prevent me from attempting to end my life for a second time. The twenty-four Tylenol 3's and the fifth of Southern Comfort I had swallowed didn't do the job as I had anticipated. While having my stomach pumped out in the emergency room, I heard somebody say, "She's got the constitution of an elephant." Not until I spoke to the psychiatrist on duty was I able to be freed from my chains. All this time I kept asking myself, "Was it worth it? Was Kathy worth all this pain?" In reply, my heart answered, "Yes," through the agony of its breaking, a pain that has taken four years to finally go away.

Four years of working full time and going to school in the evenings until I finally graduated with a degree in Social Work.

Four years of therapy, beginning with three weeks in a psychiatric hospital and ending with the advice of an excellent feminist therapist.

Four years of celibacy, deathly afraid of entering into another relationship for fear it could start the nightmare again.

Four years of changing my thinking, my way of living, my total outlook. After leaving the hospital (terrified), I sought counseling through a feminist counseling center. My therapist and I interacted well, and she helped me to begin dealing with me. It was something I had never done before. (I was always with somebody. From childhood with my family, the military with others like myself, and two long-term relationships with women who controlled my life.)

In therapy, I learned that I had assumed an adult role at a young age, due to incest and I had taken over for my mother, who wasn't strong enough to take care of herself, let alone her children. I had the tendency to suppress my emotions in order to deal with everyday problems. I kept suppressing those feelings throughout the military and my eventual coming out, becoming a police officer in the city of Detroit, and all the emotional crises I encountered. Eventually I "exploded" and my breakup with Kathy was the triggering mechanism.

I've lived alone for the main reason of getting to know myself, Jean, for the first time. I've had to learn to "feel" and not to suppress these feelings, a very difficult thing to learn. But I've done it. I now emit to others a strong, knowledgeable image and people tend to come to me with their problems. I have learned that working with people is my calling in life, so I'm now working with mothers and their children who are afflicted with AIDS. Why I chose this particular area is the fact that AIDS is a major problem and I'm not afraid of contracting the disease as many people tend to fear, a stigma I'm also trying to get rid of. We need more education in this area.

I guess my hospitalization with drug users, alcoholics, and emotionally handicapped people was the first step toward working in the social field. It made me realize how important life is. I can't help but feel, also, that God had His hand in this. I have been following a progression and will continue to do so until I accomplish what He wants me to do.

The Haunting Memory

I think of her often.
I want to tell her, but I hold back, fearing her reaction.
I remember her as if she were right here.
My memory of the way she moves is so vivid, so strong.
Her long elegant feet. Her legs strong and beautiful.
Her soft thigh, oh, how I long to run my finger
    over them again.
I can smell her sweet scent that comforted me
    and turned me on so much,
        knowing how close I was to the most tender
        part of her.
Warm, soft and oh, so wet with her juices.
The dark, curly hair protects her tender skin
    like a package and needs to be handled with care.
Her shapely hip melts into her
    strong back and shoulders,
        providing the framework for a soft stomach and
        large beautiful breast.
As I feel its firmness, I gently brush my hand
    against her nipple.
Her back is so tender to kiss, but now I remember
    the way her piercing blue eyes twinkled at me
    as she smiled.
I remember playing with her short wiry brown hair,
    as though she could see deep into my soul.
Even now her memory haunts me like a constant
    subtle breeze, never seeming to die

Karla Pettit

My lover broke up with me, saying she "needed to work things out alone" and "needed space." Two months later, she was in a new relationship and they can't be pried apart. What's going on here?

Often the phrases, "I need some time," and "I need space," or a "break" are red flags. They indicate something's going on with the relationship that the person saying these things is not saying directly to her lover. Such "lines" are often used by a partner who wants out of a relationship and doesn't know how to leave or have the courage to be honest. We need to pay attention to these clues.

Losing a Limb
by Ruby J.C. Fowler

I had lost lovers before but losing this one was like losing a limb. I felt disabled and knew that what was lost would not regenerate. Words and images clawed at the vacuum inside to get out, but when I put the pen to paper I would find it empty. Those were the hardest of times.

In the shock of an all-too-sudden stop, my life had changed. I had just ended a love affair of more than three years. It was one of those I'd imagined could last forever. Though I'd ended the relationship with words, I had really already been left months before. I'd been the primary lover to my girlfriend and the other woman was just that–the other woman, the one who gets told, "I love you but I can't be with you because I have to stay with my lover." But by a strange twist of fate, this stranger was my girlfriend's number one baby and *I* was the other woman–raw clay to be reshaped into "just a friend."

It was as if the sky had darkened and lowered its belly just above me, threatening to suck me up. I wanted to run my finger through it, until I could grab it by the guts and turn it inside out–savagely, I imagined. I wanted back into a world of sun, one that would cast shadows and warm my cold parts if I stood in the right place. The irony of the situation would rise and swell inside me, deep inside my chest like a heartbeat run amuck. Like a clock struck in tic waiting for toc, the hands around the face would begin to sweep hysterically. And I felt hysterical. "Where is toc? Come toc, so this can stop." Picture me in classic headache pose: the hands clutching the sides of the head, palm cupped over the ears, features of the face contorted, eyes pinched shut, teeth clenched. There is color in my face for the first time in a long time—red. Within the many moments that seemed to consume me in this way, I'd find it so hard to believe the relationship was over.

It was hard to believe because of the way we were with each other still. It was the way we looked into each other's faces. It was in the depth of the eyes. It was in the touch of the hand, the way the fingers traced the veins in the arm of the other, the way the lips would part on the good-night kiss. It was the sensation in the thighs and hips. I knew these things were not merely my imagination.

But when the sky bellied over me the way it did, my strength began to slip and I'd begin to forget. I would wonder if anything had been between us at all. What I believed, I feared, would be my demise. What I did not believe, I feared, was trying to kill me. I began to imagine that the tie that once bound us was just long enough now to choke the life out of anything left breathing. I feared so much, I knew so little. This was not usual in my life.

"Well," one may ask, "What about broken promises of 'forever'?" Well, there weren't any. Not this time. At forty I had already learned that "forever" can be as short as a month or as long as a few years, but not often does it blissfully leap and bound into much more than that. So I was not embittered by broken promises of forever. But girlfriend had promised not to leave me the way she had left her last lover. She had promised to keep the agreements we had so painstakingly made. We wove what I had felt was a tight web, one that would give us room to grow in any needed direction. She had promised to carry me along in her process, to reveal to me the truths of her life...blah, blah, blah. So when I found out months later that she had been sleeping with the other woman, that I had not been told of this until her hand had been forced, I felt cheated. I felt slain. My spirit had been dragged out of my life and murdered before my very eyes. I saw that though girlfriend walked the walk and talked the talk, when confronted with reality she fell one foot over the other as she stumbled from one silence to the next. I saw that truth had not been an obvious possibility. Painfully, I learned that deception was stronger than the weave of any web that I had hoped would hold us in times such as these. I was not spent by the fact of sex, but rather by active omissions. I had been betrayed by gutlessness. The greatest love, it turned out, was really only mediocre. This was the greatest sadness of all for me and I was left feeling deep in shit. Sometimes it left me feeling rather nasty.

I wanted to hate them. I wanted anger to kick in and take over the pain, hollow out the swell of my brain. But I could not and it would not. But I did think about killing one or another.

I kept a .38 at the head of my bed to ward off intruders and I certainly felt intruded upon. And as people understand crimes of passion as they understand no other, I knew the world would show me compassion. "No cold blood here," I would be able to say and be believed.

I actively imagined two rather grueling methods, each based on the flavor of my pain at the time: One was that I would go to girlfriend's house and ring the doorbell. When she opened the door, I would say nothing, though I would engage her face to face, eye to eye. Then suddenly, before there was a breath between us, I would eat my gun. I imagined blood and brains bursting from the back of my head–such stains on Steiner Street that no rain would wash away. As I tumbled down the stairs onto the street, the horror in girlfriend's face would be etched in my dead eyes forever; burned into my retinas. I would take it to the grave, the surprise in the eyes of the other. Horrible. How could I even think of it?

Actually, I couldn't think of it much, so my second idea was more palatable. I would simply track down the other woman at work. I would step behind the counter and pull the pistol from the pocket of my beige Colombo-style raincoat that I would be wearing for eccentricity's sake. Then, quick as a flash, moving so fast that no one would even notice, I would press the barrel of the gun into her chest, point it right into her heart. I would say to this woman as I watched her eyes shift and the shape of her mouth change. "This one's for the gipper." I would pull the trigger. I'm sure we would both wince at the sound. I would try to remember to make myself watch her die. Already I wondered, would a gurgle dangle deep in the throat; would I hear death rattle? Would I then shoot myself as I so often hear of? I knew that when anger comes to collect from one so spent, it's the product of push and panic, this turning of the gun on oneself, but I hoped I would just sit down and wait. I might moan and sob with face in hands as those around me danced, frantic in their horror. Perhaps I would only stare at the clock across the room, counting the minutes until the cops came.

I imagined that during the years I'd spend in prison I would use to learn math and to read music; and girlfriend would finally get to be alone, something she always said she needed to do, but never did.

But that was then and this is now, one year later. We are all still alive, regardless of how estranged or sloppy our circles might be. There are no more fantasies of hopeless homosexual "homocide." I chose life over death, though I will probably never learn math or to read music because of it. As for the other two, the other woman went back to her own girlfriend only to leave her again for someone else's; and girlfriend is still lamenting the loss of us both. I have taken no lovers since then because I knew that before I could take on the future, I had to confront the past; that before I could let anyone else into my life, I had to get one. To do that I had to be alone with the ghouls of my memories as well as the sweetness of my dreams.

I never wanted to be sentimental about sex, but for a long time I could not want it with anyone. How could I? I'd had only one heart after all, no matter how many cunts I'd like to have–only one heartbeat. It had become a dying love, this is true, twisted in its own wreckage; murdered in its sleep. Over time, it was a slow death that came too quickly nonetheless. And though I have had dreams that died with dignity, that faded away clean, and whose only traces could be found neatly in the memory–this dream lay like a scar on the skin, or break in the bone. In the end we limped away from each other, crippled by lies.

But there is always love when self-hate and anger fails you. So I remember now that my lover used to sit inside my heart, the way a seed sits inside any woman–snug, wrapped tight inside layer upon layer of heat, mush and blood. Gut inside gut. Growing, surviving pain and disorder, growing more. When we would kiss, the breath slipped past the flesh and filled us up. Like helium, it lifted us high above ourselves. Then I understood why time had brought us together.

I learned a great deal about fear, pain, and throwing myself into their apparently bottomless throats. If you believe the parachute will open, it will. And though some scar tissue will always ache in the rain, bitterness fades with the bruises if you rub it long and hard enough. If you breathe deep, your vision will clear suddenly, sometimes when you feel you are blind. The small muscles of your face will loosen. Your mouth will begin to widen, to turn up instead of down. Your jaw will drop and your scalp will rise from the hard line of your eye bone, changing the shape of your worried brow. Your senses will sharpen and you will know that you have survived.

Broken Windows, Berries, Hollywood Blvd. and a Skylight

A new road will await
formed from this old
She has said "Go now—
this was not our fate."

"Your tears will dry
and your wound will heal,"
She says "and J will be
just a faded memory—
J know how you'll feel."

This new road J approach
is empty and cold
and J am alone now
without her to hold

"You are not the first one,"
they say
A lost love is hard, yes, but
new loves await."
Ah, but J searched for my lover,
my friend and my mate—
Jt took many years of my time
only to find
that J was not hers
and she was not mine

Diane De Moon
©1991

Journal Entries
by Elaine Leeder

2/2/89

I have just spent my first truly alone evening since I found out that Jan is leaving. I feared such an evening and yet I found that I was fine with myself, that I can be by myself and be whole. An evening alone can bring me the same quiet place that being with a lover or with friends can. I found that I know how to entertain myself, that silence can bring peace, not panic, and that I can be good company for myself. This is an important learning and one that I will return to during this rocky ride I will be on for awhile. We have been together for nine years. I have been partnered for over twenty. This will be the first time I will be alone in that long. I am frightened and yet I know that I will survive this too. My emotions are a roller coaster and I need to know how to center, to find my core and my strength, to enjoy my thoughts, my warm bed in my flannel nightgown, my books, papers, phone and journals that surround me. I feel I am healing, and it will be slow, but I will survive this enormous loss and I will come out with someone and something quite important: my self.

2/6/89

Some days I am crazed. Tearful, suicidal and hopeless. Other days I see that this will pass. People say it will take over two years to heal. I can't wait that long. I am in such pain. This is worse than childbirth. This is far more painful than the death of both my father and my mother combined. I loved Jan more than myself, more than my child whom I once left for her. This experience is far greater in magnitude than anything I have ever thus far experienced. I am a walking corpse. Others look at me and react strongly to the pain they see. What will take the stab out of my heart? Another relationship, sleeping with someone perhaps. I need the pain to stop, it hurts too much.

2/10/89
Being with loving friends sure helps. I am whole here with Cleo and Ron. I am loved. Being here proves it, even if Jan loves me no more. The biking, the long talks, the hugs of kindness reach across the alienation that I most always feel.

2/21/89
I now have habits and rituals for living alone: early rising, coffee, work on my writing projects, or see a few psychotherapy clients. Then I usually swim a mile, then into the office for either office hours or teaching, more clients and then late night aloneness. My work has given me a reason to go on. Being in the classroom or helping a client can give me meaning. It takes me out of myself for awhile. For the most part I feel as if I am living in a fog, surrounded by dark, death shadows. The gloom lifts for the moments at work when I am distracted from myself, then returns immediately when the others leave my presence. Someday I hope I will feel at peace again. How will it ever come?

3/7/89
I am beginning to feel a bit better today. I have not been diminished by this experience, I have been enhanced. By losing the person closest to me I discovered myself, my strengths, my abilities to deal and survive in the world and the power that I have to carry on in the face of enormous pain. In two months I have learned to be alone and that I am not always lonely. When you open yourself lots actually comes your way. I have learned that I am resourceful and that I am attractive and appealing in the world. People respond to me when I reach out. I am fun and playful and others like that. So do I. I have learned that my work gives me enormous pleasure and pride. I have also learned that no one person should ever become as important to me as she became, that it is not healthy for me to love as deeply as I did. I have learned to hold back, to withhold a part of myself, that I need not give 250%. Maybe 85% is

fine. I must hold back some for me. Perhaps if I hold back I will not be as deeply wounded as I was by this awful experience.

3/23/89

I am in Boston with family for a conference. Being with family does not satisfy. They don't understand this kind of suffering. But the conference sure helps. I can engage with ideas, I can be smart and competent. No one here knows of my grief. Here I am a whole person with a mind. Being in Boston gives me roots and history. Here I was a student. Here I was a member of a family. Here I had many friends. Here there was Jan, but now it is my city alone once again.

4/10/89

Yesterday was the hardest day of my life. I went to the Pro-Abortion march in Washington. I was there with 600,000 and I was there alone. I ran into Jan and her new lover almost immediately. How could it be, among that many people, that I could see them? Seeing them there together, as we had been just 18 months ago for the Gay Pride March, just devastated me. I was wiped out for the rest of the day. Nothing could have been worse. I cried all day, lonely. The ephemeral quality of happiness really struck me. When we had been there together with friends it had been one of our most glorious times. Now it is gone. When will my time come again? I certainly deserve happiness. Surely it will have to come around once more. James Baldwin says that life is a waterwheel: You have to hold your nose as you go under and try to keep breathing normally when you are on top. I must stay alive till it goes up again.

4/25/89

Seeing a new woman now. It feels like a life raft. I don't know how long it will last. It feels like "transitional object" stuff to me. But it sure helps to sleep with someone, to be held, to have someone to talk to every day. I appreciate the "gift of the universe" that has come in the form of a kind and loving woman.

5/21/89

Travel is sure helping to ease the pain now. I am in San Francisco to see family and enjoy the sun. I think I am a 7 on my 10 point emotional Richter scale. It is so good to be away, not to see Jan around town, to experience myself as a free and independent woman. I felt strong. I have decided that upon my return I will cease all contact with Jan. It hurts too much to be in touch, to hear of her happiness with her new lover and not to still understand what happened and why she left me after all those years. This is such a hard decision, but one I need to make.

6/16/89

Time to end my most recent affair. I'm just not into it. I think I am not ready to be involved with someone yet. All I do is compare her to Jan and not appreciate who she is. I must be in the hummingbird phase of relationship breakup–flitting from person to activity. Time to center and be alone once more. I am more at peace there.

7/7/89

Today is my forty-fifth birthday and I am here in Harare, Zimbabwe. It is really hard to believe I did this, came to Africa all alone. Sure I am here to visit an old friend, but I had no idea what I was getting into–it could have been tse-tse flies and snakes for all I knew. Instead I have family. The whole clan adopted me and will be throwing me a birthday party tomorrow. Sixty five people are expected to greet me, a stranger and friend from the U.S. I did go to an astrologer today to hear what is to come for me. She said Jan would one day regret her decision, but that I will have moved past her and that the trust would be impossible to restore since there was such betrayal in our breakup. She said I was a "good person" who had been done wrong, but that one day justice will come and that I won't have to do it; it will come on its own. She also told me that I had come to Africa to heal but that I must return home, where the real healing will take place. The woman had insight and wisdom. I am ready to go home. I was brave and gutsy. I came here all alone to find out who I am. I found it. Now I will take the learning home, to continue the journey.

10/1/89

I have rediscovered Judaism in this new experience of myself alone in the world. This year, for the first time in twenty five, I went to the Jewish New Year services. It was wonderful. I was with loving friends who surrounded me. The ritual was familiar and yet it was new for me. This, too, will now become part of who I am. The amazing thing about this breakup is that I am finding out, often for the first time, what is important to me, just me, not the other in my life. I so appreciate the opportunity to discover all that.

11/2/89

Talked to Jan today for the first time in many months. It actually went fairly well and I recovered fairly quickly. She said she still misses me and thinks of me often. In fact, she even still loves me. She had also put herself in my position a thousand times and understands why I can't see her. We agreed that perhaps one day we will be able to be friends. For now she is out of my life, but never out of my heart.

11/24/89

On my way home from a wonderful trip to San Francisco, a most amazing thing happened. I met someone to whom I was truly attracted and we became involved. Certainly it is not a match made in heaven, but one that makes me feel great. I am into this, for the first time since Jan and I broke up. There are people out there after all. In fact, Jan is not the only woman in the world I will ever care about. She might have been the first and my most significant. But now I see that each woman I encounter can enhance my life, each in a unique and important way. I never imagined that I could feel as good as I do right now. It has been many months but time and life experiences surely do bring healing. I am glad to be alive.

12/4/89

Just spent a wonderful weekend in Washington, D.C. with Roccena who had flown in on a work-related trip from San Francisco. We did a most liberating thing, one that really made me smile and feel free. After a long walk together we went to the very street corner on which I had encountered Jan and her lover on the day of the march. There I was kissed and held and told that I did not have to be a slave to the pain of that day, that the memory of it was now countered by the loving treatment shown me this cold day in December. There is joy and happiness after break up. Often it feels long in coming, as if it will never appear again. But it does return and with it comes hope for love once again.

8/13/90

I have ended my "interlude" with Roccena. It was good while it lasted, but I am now ready to be in a relationship. It is time to move on. Being with her was wonderful and painful. It wasn't as deep and meaningful as my time with Jan, but I both grew and learned. It was not love but it sure helped me in the healing that was needed to pull myself completely away from Jan. Being with Roccena taught me lots, including about my own sexuality and who else I could be. I am pleased for having been involved with her and I am pleased for having the strength to end something when it is not quite right for me.

12/16/90

I have been alone and really unpartnered for almost two years. There have been a few affairs, but certainly no committed relationship in my life. Now I am in dating mode, meeting lots of new women and enjoying my freedom and independence. Sure there are moments when I long to be with my partner, but for the most part I am happy with my life and who I am. This woman who was once a walking corpse is now a thriving, competent, attractive and lovable human being. I really have no idea what will come next. Will I remain alone for awhile, will I have affairs, will I fall in love and live "happily ever after?" That is highly unlikely, but there is ever the hope for even that. The learning from this experience has been vast and deep. I would never have chosen to learn in this way, but I was forced to deal with it and in the process I grew more than I could ever have imagined. Now I have come to see life as a long path on which I travel alone. Sometimes people will be there to walk with me, for awhile. Then their paths will veer off and I will walk alone again. Perhaps there will be another to walk with me, one who might stay awhile. Until that time I will walk on alone and enjoy the sense of self and peace that has emerged and has become an integral part of my life.

My lover and I own property and expensive items. Now we're breaking up and fighting about who gets what. We thought we'd be together forever and never made legal arrangements. She's driving me crazy with her demands, but I don't want to just give in and lose things I cherish and paid half for. What can I do?

 First of all, whenever there's property other than personal property (furnishings, books, etc.) you need to draw up a contract with an attorney who specializes in domestic partnerships. Oftentimes when we break up, there is added stress when you've shared property and personal items. Memories and sentiments can provide a struggle of power. It is important to recognize what you're willing to give up is not the material, but the fear of letting go of the relationship. For example: You bought a teapot together while on a trip to Europe. It's an antique, and you both love it, but—it's an antique, and you collect antiques, while your (ex) lover loves tea time. Should you give in to her whims and feel cheated or resentful, or should you hold out and feel victorious that you got your way? The beginning of a breakup is not the time to divide effects up other than personal ones like clothes, records, etc.; there is too much emotion. It's advisable to delay this process and work it out through a mediator, or wait until you're both more certain of what you want.

Strength, Hope and Recovery
by Anne Wolf-Grey

My breakup with Laurie was one of the most devastating times of my life. Laurie was my first Lesbian relationship; she was my first real relationship, period. I had dated a few men, but would always back away when sex entered the picture. I just wasn't interested in sex with them...or dating them, for that matter.

Laurie had a special role to fulfill in my life. She came along at a time when I was ready to begin to confront those old feelings I had tried to repress for a long time; my attraction for other women.

She became the closest friend I had ever had. As our friendship grew, we both started gradually admitting and realizing the depth of our affection for one another.

Laurie introduced me to my sexuality and to being a lesbian. It was a wonderful introduction. She was gentle and loving. I was not her first relationship. I fell "head over heels" in love with her.

Making love with Laurie felt so right and so natural. She was a wonderful kisser. I felt connected with parts of myself I had missed, and yet hadn't even known were there. At times I would feel very at-one with her.

We had known each other for almost two years before we became involved. When we started getting involved, I had been in counseling for about a year and was just beginning to deal with issues of family alcoholism. I had in that one year, begun to really know myself. Forgotten interests became new passions, and for the first time in my life, I had a very strong sense of direction. I had dreams, and was on the way to making them come true.

One evening, on my way to school, I saw the most magnificent sunset–a column of orange light extending from the horizon up. I had never seen such a phenomenon as that before–or after. I felt the presence of God and the importance of that moment. I got out of the car and stood watching the sunset. To my surprise, something very deep inside me said yes, that I was willing to make a commitment to Laurie, and to this relationship, no matter what. I felt very peaceful.

But peace became a rare experience as our relationship went on. Laurie was the only person I was "out" to. I was still trying to accept myself. I had no other support, whereas she had several friends who she could confide in. We became isolated. Mixed in with the joy of validation of myself and my sexuality, and the deep love I felt for Laurie, was tremendous fear. I had so much internalized homophobia that fear began to color every aspect of my life. In addition, neither of us, myself especially, had any boundaries. We became co-dependent.

She was the giver, who appeared to enjoy giving, and I was the needy one. The taker. I can't speak for her, but I think she grew tired of giving and resented it.

After a few short months, our relationship ended. She had stayed in contact with her first lover and felt there was a lot to resolve. She went to California to see her ex, to try to resolve what she was feeling. She came back with her love for this woman renewed. Two days after her return, she told me she couldn't see me anymore. I was devastated. I hadn't wanted her to go to California, and I began immediately to blame myself: "If only I hadn't 'let' her go," etc.

We talked several times after that night. I had heard all the stuff about how common it is for lesbians and their former lovers to be friends. That's what she seemed to want with me. I thought that very unfair to me. She got a new lover and got to keep an old friend. I got a friend I no longer trusted and lost my lover. Every time I thought of her with someone else, I felt nauseous. About a month after our breakup, we stopped talking. The last time I heard from her, she said she was moving to California to be with her new/old love.

I had intuitively known that would happen, but it still hurt a lot. I told her to drop me a postcard sometime to let me know how she was doing. She was very hurt by that, and I've never heard from her since.

The first few days after the breakup were the hardest. I was suicidal. It was a very difficult summer anyway: my brother was getting a divorce, my mom was drinking heavily, and my dad was critically ill.

An awful time. Ironically, it was Laurie who kept me from really seriously considering suicide. She had two friends, one of them her former lover, who had tried to kill themselves over her. Laurie's ex-lover told me that early on in our relationship, as if to warn me. I'd vowed to prove her wrong when told. I must have known on some level that this wouldn't work out.

I processed with my counselor, who I "came out" to immediately. That was really frightening. I thought she would try and "fix" me. But she was very supportive.

I cried a lot. I did rage work, punching cushions until they were destroyed. I took up running. It was the only way I knew to get all that pent-up anger and energy out of my body. I took things one day at a time. I had a job that required a lot of energy, so I used that as an outlet, too.

There were really lonely times. Part of me wanted her back, but most of me wasn't willing to compromise for her again. With my counselor's encouragement, I allowed myself to really feel my loneliness. It became less and less frightening and overwhelming.

I had been in counseling for Adult Children of Alcoholics issues. I began attending ACOA meetings, a 12-step group for people who grew up in dysfunctional families. It was awkward at first, and I resented going. But soon I found a real home there with other people who understood me. I did not come out to them. I did not share the details of the breakup, other than to make it sound like a male/female relationship and calling "him" a jerk. But ACOA helped me with a lot of my basic issues.

I made a commitment to myself not to get seriously involved with anyone for at least a year. In Alcoholics Anonymous, it's called "doing your year." A year seemed like a very long time, especially when all I wanted to do was be in another relationship. But the more I focused on myself and my needs, the less I wanted to deal with anyone else or a relationship.

I learned to discern needs and wants, and to identify them. I learned to take care of my own needs so I didn't look to someone outside of me to take care of me. I defined what I wanted in a relationship. I learned about my strengths. I learned about boundaries and set appropriate ones for me in all areas of my life. I set up boundaries for an intimate relationship before I was in one. It was much easier to do than in the midst of passion. And then, after five months, it happened.

As things often work, I guess, when I wasn't looking for a relationship is when I met the woman I am going to spend the rest of my life with! We met at an ACOA meeting. We work our "programs" individually and work on our relationship together. We are two healthy women in the strongest relationship I've ever heard of.

I did stick to my boundary of no heavy involvement for a year. In fact, we waited more than a year. One of my dreams, even before being with Laurie, was to move to the West Coast and pursue my career. I needed to move. We had a solid year of friendship behind us when we decided to become physically intimate. And we did that only after she decided that she would also move. Three months later, I moved to Portland, Oregon. Susan moved out three months later. Today we found our dream home and will be moving in soon.

There were no financial losses when Laurie and I broke up. There were no children. We weren't living together, although I wanted that badly. But there was a lot of loss for me. I lost a friend I really valued. I lost my first love. I lost the false security of denying who I was sexually. After Laurie, I couldn't doubt any longer that I was a lesbian. I lost bits and pieces of myself. Laurie was a professional artist. I was an artist, too, but untrained. I was afraid to pursue my interest in art, afraid of her condemnation or fear of competition. I had also compromised my West Coast dreams. I wanted to live in Oregon. She liked sun, however, and wouldn't move any place so rainy. I started to think about California, and forgot Oregon altogether.

It's two years since the breakup, and I'm glad it happened. I am in the relationship of my dreams with someone committed to me and the relationship. I am drawing again, and I am in the midst of a period of creativity like I've never imagined. And I'm living in Oregon.

I think of Laurie often and usually fondly now. I miss her. Sometimes I miss her a lot. A good deal of the rage, hurt and feelings of abandonment are gone. I am thankful she was a part of my life, even if for a short time. And I pray for her, wherever she is, that she finds the health and happiness I am discovering. And I mean it.

My First Real Love
by Jodi Silverman

I had thought Michelle was my first love, but she was abusive to me, her family and herself. She had a drug problem and was quite unhappy. I was fortunate that she broke up with me, but I didn't think so at the time. I loved Michelle, and I thought I'd never recover.

Preceding the breakup, Michelle befriended a woman named Robin. I was shocked when Michelle blurted out, "I'm in love with Robin, not you!" I cried and cried. I couldn't sleep, I couldn't eat. I couldn't think. It was as if she'd died. I shivered. We'd been together five years.

I tortured myself, driving to Robin's apartment to see if Michelle's car was there. I wanted to know if she was sleeping at Robin's. I'd also look for Robin's car at Michelle's house. I called her in the early morning to see *how* she answered the phone.

At the same time, it was extremely difficult for me to work for the same company as Michelle. I worked at the reception desk, intercepting and monitoring all calls. When she would get a call, I'd listen on the extension. It was pure hell.

About a month later, I joined the Gay and Lesbian group at my college. I became president of the group. With new strength, I went for my Master's degree and got to the point where I felt I wanted to give love another try. I placed a personal ad in a newspaper and met Loretta.

We've been together four and a half beautiful years now. I bought a condominium in Connecticut with Loretta. I'm receiving as well as giving unconditional love.

I realized that my first love is Loretta. Michelle was an obsession, not love, and I thank her for freeing me to be in a truly loving relationship.

I'm a social worker. Friends turn to me when they face breakups. This is what I tell them:

- ♥ Allow yourself to experience the pain, but don't wallow in it;

- ♥ Go out. Join groups. Force yourself to join an organization or team;

- ♥ Find someone to discuss the pros and cons of *your* part in the past relationship;

- ♥ Rediscover yourself;

- ♥ When you feel okay being alone with yourself, start looking for Ms. Right. She *is* out there;

- ♥ Remember–good things can come out of seemingly bad situations;

- ♥ Be patient. Everyone has her own time frame. It's impossible to say how long it will take for you to get over her, but you will!

The vivid juxtaposition framed
that night...

the moon full
provided a visionary path
of two lovers,

known strangers   cheek-to-shoulder,
in beautiful sleep.   In beautiful night.

In the Creation,
born to us.

If I could witness that moon again—
my love,

I would take you in to the night.

                                        Jessica Fair Stevens

Will I ever get over the hurt and pain of feeling disappointed that our relationship didn't last?

 It's both my professional and personal experience that we do get over the loss of a relationship. Some of the suggestions I use are to keep a journal, write letters to your ex which you either mail or keep, and maintain distance while going through the healing process. In time, all things heal and we can make it happen faster when we make the effort. Breaking up can be a time of renewal, getting to know who you are and what you really want.

Breakup
by Ruth Mountaingrove

After thirteen years of living together, sharing our ideas, building our lives together, she turned to me one day and said she no longer wanted to be in a couple. I was extremely shocked at the time and when I think about it, still am. No, I would not say I got over it, anymore than I ever got over the deaths of my two children, or my parents, or my two favorite aunts. Though as I think of it now, when all my children turned 18, I got over my divorce.

It has been six years now. I have had other lovers, but not companion as she was. Other lovers are supposed to help heal, to give you back a feeling of worth, and they do. And your own direction that you give to your life gives you a feeling of worth too. But companions are rare. We were only two years apart in age. We knew the same songs, though we rarely sang them–lyrics were so sexist. We had not had the same experience growing up. Her father was a professional, mine a letter carrier. So our opportunities and privileges were different. We both had graduated from college. She had gone on to graduate school and was professional by the time I met her. I'd been a high school teacher and after my divorce had taken a blue collar job. We both had discovered feminism at the same time on the East Coast. I was involved with NOW when I met her. She directed me to real action–the Women's Liberation Movement.

This belief in and involvement with women sustained our own involvement, our own love and caring for each other. I felt that sister-hood/feminism was the keystone of our being together. We were build-ing a new woman's world.

We were not an ideal couple. We would go for a long period of time stretching and tearing the fabric that held us together, but then we could sit down and talk and work out what was irritating, angering, anguishing the other woman. And we really worked at it, because of course being such close companions we each had stuff that annoyed the other.

There is no magic formula for getting over a breakup. After six months of trying to accept that which was obvious to everyone else (she took a lover during that time and I took two), I left the land we shared and went traveling. That is one way to handle a breakup. Leave the town or city where you both have lived and where everything reminds you of her. Go looking for a new life. I did that. After months of traveling, and even going back to help take care of the land, within a year I had settled in an apartment in a small college town by the sea. Begin again. I did that. Decided to go back to school. Put all my energy into that and got an MA in Art. Became a full-fledged artist. Was so busy going to school, took such a demanding schedule, I didn't have time for regrets or sadness, though they would surface now and then in a vague depression, in the feeling that I was skating at times on very thin ice.

I have continued writing and painting. I work with various organizations, some feminists, some lesbian, some neither. I have made my way in the "real" world. But I have no companion as she was. No one to turn to in the middle of the night and share an idea with. We once said that no one could really work with us because some our best talks were in bed. That's where we got some of our best ideas.

So, no, I have not got over the breakup nor has she. Neither of us has found someone to share our lives with on a day-to-day basis. Perhaps at our age we won't. When I suggested recently that I come back and do some work I needed to do on the land, and live there for a two-week period, she became quite upset. Didn't know whether she could handle this or not. Didn't know how it would be if we were both on the land together. This after six years during which time I have rarely been there. One of the complications is that we own this land together. We share the cost of the taxes and land upkeep. She lives there. I do not. And one of the problems is that while she spent probably the last two years of our living together examining all the pros and cons of continuing in that dyad, she did not share any part of this with me. So when it was presented as her decision, I had not had a part in it at all. Hence the shock at the time of the announcement. The disbelief.

I think it is not just the complexities of owning land but the fact of our names being linked in the feminist subculture, folk heras so to speak, that has made it difficult for women who have since become our lovers. It is as though we have broken up, we trail the ghosts of each other.

She is still my partner in the land. My lovers know this. They resent this and sometimes are jealous. And they resent coming across a footnote in a book they are reading that links our names. We are part of feminist herstory. I try to put myself in my current lover's place. How would I feel if my lover still owned land with former companion, still wrote letters to her, took me to visit her land and her, still got hurt by her or angry? I think I would say to her, "Honey, call me when it's over." Her lovers may have the same impulse.

So, no, it isn't over. The dragon sleeps most of the time. When either of us disturbs it, it rumbles in its lair. You cannot put that much time and energy into being together and then shut it off or bury it. Perhaps in thirteen years, who knows? I know how deep the hurt is. How unbelieving a part of me is even today. The hurt of being left. I have been both a leaver and a left one. The leaver, too, has to come to an understanding in herself as to why she's leaving. It is the easier of the two positions but it is not easy.

Time has helped to some degree to heal, and distance has helped too. But breakups don't just involve the couple, they involve friends who have been friends of the dyad. Now they either take sides or withdraw from both. Lesbian friends did help at the time of the breakup. I can remember a massage from one, many nights of cuddling from another. A reminder from another that there was life after my companion. I remember being held while I cried out my pain. Being reminded by another that other women were attracted to me. That didn't seem possible at the time. I remember lots of hugs from my writing group. Two of my friends had a three day spiritual retreat and invited me to share it with them. We went to the ocean to be soothed with her sounds and her beauty. I am grateful for such tenderness and caring. Friends cannot change facts but they can ease them. Other friends invited me to visit. That is when I began to travel.

When she first told me about wanting more space I suggested counseling and we did that, but when one partner is determined to be finished counseling is not even Band-Aid help. And I have to say that when my companion suggested counseling a year before the breakup,

I was opposed to it, feeling this meant that we couldn't handle our own affairs ourselves which we had been able to do up to that time, or so I thought.

There were disagreements we never resolved, it's true. We maneuvered around them, we buried them by mutual consent because they were impossible to deal with. That is the way of life. It isn't perfect even though we wish it were. And I feel that this wish–that everything were the way we wanted it–was part of the breakup.

On the other hand, there are women who have the need to move on without (sob) you. And no matter what you do, she will move whether you think this is the time or not. There was that in my companion's decision. Why she couldn't move with me is still a mystery to me. But she needed a drastic change, and I was it.

So, no, I'm still not through the breakup. I enjoy my freedom of living alone, but I miss the companionship that comes of making a life together. There are the little things I miss. The hug in the morning, preparing and eating meals together, hugs during the day, cuddling, working on projects together. We did a lot of carpentry and solving problems not related to our being a couple, like getting the angle right for the roof. And I enjoyed the fire and excitement we brought to our discussions of feminist concerns. Living alone, primarily, for the last six years, meant many fewer hugs, practically no cuddling, and seldom eating with someone else. My pursuits are almost all lone ones: working in my studio, writing articles and poetry, reading, going on walks. I have to belong to groups to be with other women, or get some of that camaraderie at work, and balance that with my friends as well as I can. (I miss my companion.) I have found no one to replace my missed companion. Her way of being with me has given me a certain standard to look for. This is not fair to other women but there it is. A good companion is rare.

While I have healed a great deal, and the dragon sleeps, I am not yet through the breakup. This doesn't mean I obsess. There are days, maybe even weeks, when I don't think of her at all. But someone who has that much impact in your life will probably never be forgotten. And when I pick up a magazine and there is an article by her, or someone tells me that she heard her read a paper, or says that she met her at a women's music festival, or I receive a phone call from some women who are thinking of living in my community and they got my number from her–then the remembering of how well we worked together comes flooding back.

I have had advice on how to move on: cut all ties, sell my half of the land to her, move all my stuff out of there into storage. Now she lives with my ghost. My desk in the office looks just as I left it five years ago. My books are still on the bookshelves, my darkroom is still in need of cleaning. When there is a serious emergency, she still calls me.

The trouble is: I don't want to sell my land. For me it spells security, just as my savings account does. A foundation for my life. And I have no room for my things. I live in a one room apartment on a limited income; storage is expensive. But more than that, the wiping out of the other woman in the breakup is an artificial act. She will always be with you, in your memory and in your heart. And you cheat yourself of all the good memories, the good feelings, and the good times you had together, if you wipe her out of your thoughts. Perhaps it is these feelings of companionship, being good friends, that move lesbian women to break up or to go back to being friends after a certain amount of time has elapsed. And it may help to heal a breakup. How can you go on thinking those awful thoughts about her when you are enjoying being with her, even though under other circumstances?

But in my case at least this does not mean that I want to be back on that dyad again. Only that I'm open to another that would have the same close intellectual stimulation, the same physical and emotional tenderness and perhaps, in the beginning, the same high passion. This is a high order, I have probably a not very original idea that we never get over those we have let into our hearts. Frances, my friend from high school; Jef in college; Florence, whose friendship spanned my married life and beyond; Jean, my companion of thirteen years, and one or two lovers since then–will be with me until I die, as will some very special friends. Why would I want to forget them? They enrich my life. And possibly the lovers who break your hearts are the ones you remember longest.

This relatively calm appraisal does not reflect the anger, hurt, depression, dissolution, desolation, emptiness, insomnia, loss of appetite, fear, desperation, crying, screaming, self-destroying, suicidal feelings, the nausea that go with any breakup where you are the left one, and I speak from my own experience. It does reflect the knowledge that time and distance do heal, just as old folk wives wisdom tells us.

When the breakup comes, and the initial knowledge that it is over, it is like a death, only her ghost still walks alive in the world. Still this is death and there is mourning to do. I was bereaved of her. I wanted there to be the same loving between us. I wanted to move back to where we had been together. I wanted. I wanted. I wanted. And I was angry at her for having died to me. It was not a clean death. It was ragged, slow, lingering. She would cuddle me for 10 minutes, or as long as she could, then go away for 24 hours, coming back to hold me the next day. My body felt as though I had been physically beaten across the shoulders, neck and back. My journals of that time are so painful I still can't read them. But that was in the throes of the agony, and whether I liked it or not, miles and years dull the pain. Still, memories of those throes make me cautious. I am not the innocent I was then.

And while I have had other women lovers and we have loved each other, one or the other of us has not had any wish to live together for more than a few days at a time. It isn't age that raises caution, it is the experiencing of freedom of doing what you want to whenever you want to, and being who you are without compromise, that I would have a great deal of trouble giving up. So far I have not met another woman like my former companion. Was it because we had both been heterosexual before we became lovers with each other that we were so comfortable together? Did we stay together as long as we did because we had stayed that long in our marriages? We were both delighted to have each other. We had both loved other women from afar. We had lived with men who had little comprehension of how sexist they were. Who had little understanding of what it might mean to work out what might be bothering one or the other of us. Who did a great deal of talking but very little giving. Here was another human being who could be nurturing, too. We were amazed by each other, and very pleased.

A friend of mine uses the image of weaving to describe this process of unraveling. When we come together, she says, we join our two weavings together and then, at the time of parting, these joinings, deep in the weave, are pulled out again, and the two weavings separate. This process is very painful. Or she likens breakup to a wound that has healed over but is broken open by each breakup. She feels from her own experience that she never heals. Another of my friends whom I shared this paper with asked me if I had written any unsent letters and showed me a sheaf of hers. That is how she worked out for herself her confusion and bewilderment at being left. I said I used my journal for the same purpose.

There is another aspect to my breakup. It is possible that I, on a largely unconscious level, engineered it. That something in me needed to be free. And through health problems, which also resulted in impatience and anger on my part, and unkindness, and even rudeness, I may very well have determined what my partner eventually decided. I, who had been her emotional sounding board, was worn out for being used in that way. I found myself saying things in reply in my head, though not out loud. But we had and still have a telepathic connection, so how could she not know on some level what I was thinking? But I, myself, was too afraid to make the change even though I needed to make it to grow. Of course, I knew there would be pain. How could I make that choice consciously? So I didn't. And there was pain and the blackness and fear of the unknown when I was forced into that change, just as I had known there would be. On the other hand, I was alive and not bored.

And with the breakup came illness. A very serious flu. I wonder if sometimes we don't have to burn this dis-ease out of ourselves, rather like an alchemical fire, to transmute the lead of the status quo into the gold acceptance. I was scoured by this fire I nearly died from and as I came back to life I was able to move on. Able to plan on an intellectual level my future without my companion. To open myself on an emotional level to many women. To slowly build my life again with new connections, new interests.

Why do I mention all this? Because to be fair (my companion would say there is no such thing as being fair) I need to accept my own part in the breakup. My own fear and anger. My deep unwillingness to admit our love or at least our passion had died. When we first became lovers, we agreed that when we no longer had deep feelings for each other we would go our separate ways grateful for what we had had. We would not let our connection die a slow death. But then, when it did, we did not have the courage or the energy to keep that agreement. We were totally involved with day to day practical needs.

It has been good to write my mullings on breakup. To look again at what changed my life so radically, pushing me back into a heterosexual world from my separatist new world I was building with my companion, or at least thought I was building. Buiding with other lesbians who had our vision. For the past four years in academia I have to deal largely with men. The percentage of women, let alone lesbians, was minuscule. My vision seems impossible. My women's spirituality in abeyance. But there are some new beginnings. In my paintings, I am using goddess symbols from 5000 B.C., bringing my vision into my art. And perhaps trust can build again, is building. Perhaps there can be another companion. No, I have not got over the breakup but writing about it has been healing. While I enjoy my privacy as much as the next woman, I feel we need to tell each other about our own breakups so that we can share what we have discovered and learn we are not alone in our pain. In this sharing way, too, we can build our lesbian culture.

Healing from Her, onto Myself
by Ryma Birch

"Mourning is a process of letting go," my therapist told me. It is not dying. Almost two years later, I feel blessed to understand his words.

My coming out relationship was magnetic–I felt sucked in and later unable to get out of the quagmire. Though I had had two previous lesbian relationships, I had not crossed the bridge into Lesbian Territory until I met Lynn. Our astrological charts showed an uncanny match if we wanted truth-telling and challenge to transcend our limitations. The stars, however, can paint only one picture. Almost immediately, the dynamism in our relationship became dynamite and we slowly tore each other apart. Eventually we came to grips with the nightmare, and we separated. We had sacrificed too much of ourselves for the hopes of our souls.

I was sailing uncharted water in the ending of an awful relationship. In spite of my ex's demonic side with me, I missed her enthusiasm, our dreams, the reflection of my own potential. But even more, I felt the loss of myself in the hell I traveled through to come into the light. Healing was excruciatingly slow, one step at a time. One poem at a time. One entry in my journal. One drawing. Day after day, week after week, bolstered up in one counseling session after another, I sorted out my jumbled feelings and found courage to express them. The first stage was getting clear, tuning into my inner self, responding to concrete challenges she presented (including harassment); it was based on the addictions model of recovery. It was hard to sever the caring cord as I was advised to do, and to accept that a woman lover was abusive. Fortunately, I was sane enough to see she didn't merit understanding from me if I was terrified that I couldn't protect myself from her. Reading of similar breakups and listening to others' experiences empowered me as I sought answers to all my questions. I dared to trust myself again.

Eventually I chose a geographical cure, to experience the support of family. Even though they couldn't really understand what I had suffered, we expanded our coming out process as a family in my need. I felt loved and secure again. Distance helped immeasurably–I no longer was confronted daily with memories in my house. I no longer felt the threat of invasion of my space. Time, too, afforded me opportunities to meet new people, share lessons and reflect on where I had come from. Eventually, I even began to feel some warmth towards her again.

The second stage of my healing, a feminist-artist approach, came when I decided it was time to face my body terror of her presence. I had returned to our town for the summer; she lived only three blocks away and had tried to establish contact.

I re-read May Sarton's description of a wrongful lesbian relationship: "[Hilary] was once more in the presence of the Muse, the crucial one, the Medusa who had made her understand that if you turn Medusa's face around, it is your own face. It is yourself who must be conquered...the creative person, the person who moves from an irrational source of power, has to face the fact that this power antagonizes. Under all the superficial praise of the 'creative' is the desire to kill."

I then remembered Kali, the Hindu goddess. In order to face the wildness Lynn represented, I had to depersonalize her and see her energy in a larger, symbolic framework. I could then write about my mythological journey in the relationship and draw from a deeper source. Joseph Campbell's description of Kali fit Lynn, and I felt vindicated:

"Bondage and liberation are both of her making. She is self-willed and must always have her own way. She is full of bliss." I knew that in the beginning I had looked to her for liberation from my own eating disorder, that I wanted to experience my own bliss. I could not envision the price I would have to pay for coming close to her. Kali was "the most terrifying aspect of Devi, with a thirst for blood and sacrificial human killings, whose stomach is a void and so can never be filled."

Although I knew the Goddess had Her dark side, I had to translate that evil into my own life. Once I could place our story in a larger human story, I was prepared to look her in the eye (when next we met) and begin to ponder the best way to approach the Bad Fairy. I wanted to destroy the power she still held over me.

And it happened: she did ring the doorbell again. Although I was taken by surprise once more, my body did not freeze! I walked with her to a neutral zone, and we talked, after two years of silence. I looked at her and saw everything I had ever felt–the mirror of our relationship– and kept breathing. Being able to stay centered in her presence was real victory for me. I felt unhooked and free. In our brief conversation, I could sense that she, too, had grown. I was glad for her sake. I also knew that she was not yet ready for any healing that would involve me, as much as either of us might want otherwise.

As I look back on the two years of severance, I see how I experienced my separateness from her only as I was able to give to my Self what I needed; to truly mourn the loss of our relationship. In the early stages of our separation, I was overwhelmed with intense feelings related to her wounded acting out. I didn't understand how self care actually helped me to mourn. My therapist saw that I was in danger of confusing mourning and dying, of identifying with the relationship. When I wasn't able to receive any more from Lynn, it was too easy to want to escape my pain to avoid dwelling on it. If I shut down my feelings, it was hard for me to take in nourishment from any source, especially from myself.

By learning to discern and attend to my own needs acutely, I strengthened my boundaries and began to face who I was and am and who we were together. I cleared away the debris to get to firm ground. I let go of the illusions and clearly saw what was worth mourning. It may be quite awhile before my dreams of her are not nightmares. They are my trusted barometers to let me know I am not yet done healing. I know now that recovery can't have a timetable. I don't know how long the road is. I do know that mourning is a procession towards new life and the full power of the sun.

My lover left me and I'm just not myself. I thought I'd support her need to leave, but most of the time I feel irritable and lethargic at the same time. What's going on with me? What can I do?

 Don't be surprised to feel deceived, sad, betrayed, abandoned and jealous. You might think your love wasn't unconditional after all. You might lose your sexual interest, emotional interest, and isolate yourself from others since your relationship legitimized your sexual identity and status as a lesbian. But at this stage you have ample opportunities for emotional growth. The loss is a catalyst for change and gives you the perfect time to build a relationship with yourself and to learn about yourself with more understanding. You can gain insight, self confidence, and expand social networks and relationships. You can do the things you always wanted to do, but never got around to doing.

Beyond the Pain
of Your Leaving

Awake in the night
oh, answers and sight
the blessing of wisdom unbound

in touch with my being
feeling, meaning
gazing past darkness into the light

hath no place for fears
no reason for tears
if remember i always my light

for light be secure
no shadow can near
the brightness that love doth possess

and light be my friend
no need to pretend
forever my light to endure.

Anita L. Pace

Signs Your Relationship May Be in Trouble
by Dakota Sands, MSW

♥ Communication changes–Not talking about what's going on.

♥ Lots of arguments–Excessive nit-picking, *i.e.*, money.

♥ Sexual inactivity or decline in sexual involvement.

♥ Sleeping in separate bedrooms with justified excuses. Excessive consumption of alcohol, drugs or food.

♥ Withdrawal of interaction–*i.e.*, not sharing activities together.

♥ Enjoyment of time spent with friends more than with your partner.

♥ Lack of trust–*i.e.*, questioning your partner or being questioned by your partner for every move made.

♥ Having an affair.

♥ Having an affair and not being honest with your partner.

♥ Holding back anger and building resentment.

Part II

Loss Without Choice—

When She Dies

After many disappointing relationships, I thought I could never have happiness in this life. Then I met a woman with whom I had nearly seven wonderful years together. After she died at a young age, my old thoughts came back. I'm afraid to ever love again. I finally wasn't left by another, but still had my lover taken away. Are some people just destined to never have long-lasting happiness with another?

 It's very painful to lose someone through death. Where there is hope for a reconciliation after a breakup, there's not after the finality of death. And certainly a part of our loving spirit seems to have died along with one's partner/lover. How fortunate you both were to know one another and experience life together. Thinking about how frightening it is to be with someone else is a normal fear after such a loss. But no one is destined to be alone if they recognize they have the ability to love another person and they are willing to take the risk again. You have a choice in your own destiny.

Facing Life Without You

Not sure if I can make it
Facing life without you
This was the last thing
I thought I'd ever have to do
Face life without you.

Friends and life are so precious
Yet we take them both for granted
It's only when we lose them
We know just what they meant to us.

When the phone rings
Should be you saying hi
Still expect to see you
Walking thru my door
Just can't believe you're gone
Oh, why'd you have to go and die?

J thought we'd grow old together
We'd laugh and share in our
memories
We had some grand times
and our share of bad times
But we had something special
My friend and me.

Jm trying to be strong
Cuz thats how she'd want it
But the road is rocky
And the days lonely and long
How can J pull thru
How can J do it
My friend?

Jm so lost without you
J'll try babe, for you, J'll try
Jts not gonna be easy tho
Facing life without you.

Doralyn Moran
July 3, 1980

Life, Death, Reality, Life Again
by Doralyn Moran

M y life, I imagine, has been like millions of other women in ways. But although I had boyfriends in high school, I also was attracted to certain girlfriends, having feelings I didn't understand. In the 1940s, I wasn't very sharp about such feelings most people of my generation had never heard of.

I was a virgin when I married at age 20. I wasn't in love, but I was infatuated with my handsome husband, amazed he'd chosen me. Yet on my wedding night, I made quite a discovery. "This" was not for me! I felt repulsed and didn't feel much better for the following 17 years of marriage and three children later. I knew there must be something out there for me, but I didn't know what. And I knew I couldn't go on living this lie, feeling so miserable.

I'd heard about "queers," "homos" and all the other nasty names, but that couldn't be me. Every once in a while, I felt my heart leap at being close to a female friend or co-worker, but I couldn't figure out what that meant.

I left my husband in 1969 and moved to Southern California with my children. I found a good job in medical assisting and office management and was very happy for two years. I was content to go to work, come home, fix dinner, go to bed, and start all over again the next day.

In 1971, it was my job to interview prospective registered nurses for a position in our office. I'd interviewed many nice, qualified women. Then Joanne walked in. We spoke a few minutes, my heart pounding, my throat dry, and my hands shaking. I managed to get through the interview without making a fool of myself. I wanted to hire her. Fortunately, she was also the most qualified. I had this feeling that I'd die if I never saw her again.

After working together for many months, we became best friends. I loved her so much. I'd never felt this way before. I didn't have a clue what to do. She was married and very well known in the community, with many friends.

I was extremely nervous. I had headaches, panic attacks, and lost weight. I felt desperate. I didn't have anyone to talk to. Hell, I hadn't even admitted what these feelings meant to myself. All I knew was that I'd fallen in love with a woman.

After nearly a year of sheer torture, I called Joanne one night and said I had to see her. I was terrified. I told her I had to tell her something, but it would have to be outside, in the dark, in the car. She thought I was losing my mind, but agreed.

We sat in the car about 10 minutes. I shook. I smoked about eight cigarettes. Joanne became impatient. "Come out with it or I'm going back in the house...For God's sake, what can be so bad?" she asked.

"I love you," I blurted.

"I love you, too, kiddo," she said.

"I don't think you understand," I said. "I am in love with you. You mean more to me than life and I have feelings for you I don't fully understand. But I want you in a way I've never wanted anyone. I want to make love with you." (Of course, I had no idea to go about this.)

The weight of the world was off my shoulders once I told her. I didn't even care if I were ridiculed or if she never wanted to see me again.

Joanne looked at me and took my hand. "You idiot. Don't you know I love you, too, and I want you the same way? I want to spend the rest of my life with you." We kissed and I felt pleasure, fire, and desire that I'd never felt before.

There was nothing we could do about the situation at that time. We stole a few kisses and embraces for months, and held hands at the movies. But she had a husband and a 14 year old daughter. I lived in my home with three daughters and two grandchildren. Jo and I lived in fear of losing our jobs, but she told her husband about us and asked him to leave the house. Their marriage had never been a happy one, and he was more than happy to do so.

I had to take the next step. It's been more than 18 years, but I'm still struggling with the guilt of having sent my younger children to live with their father and his wife. I made up a lie that I was drinking too much and (not a lie) going through a tough time with our youngest daughter. It broke my children's hearts and that has been painful for me, too. The scene still haunts me, but I just couldn't bring them into the relationship I was entering into.

I moved in with Jo. The first two times we slept together, she wanted to make love. I was terrified and said I wasn't ready. The truth is, I didn't know what to do. I thought I'd ruined everyone's life so I could be with Jo, and then I was too frightened to "do" anything. So on the third night, I just looked at her, felt the love, and let it take over. Whatever I did, it felt right, good and loving. It was wonderful. In my 42 years, I'd never known how beautiful it is to make love with someone I loved.

Jo's daughter accepted me and took me in as a loved one in her family. As long as her mom was happy, everything was okay with her. She never hid the truth from her friends and never kept them from coming to the house. As a result, we always had a house full of teenagers.

Jo and I bought wedding bands and exchanged our own private vows that we would be together until "death do us part." We didn't know death would part us so soon. Jo had diabetes. The disease made her fragile. In our eight years together, I took care of her as best I could. But on March 19, 1980, Joanne passed away suddenly from complications of diabetes.

I felt my life ended that day. When a person loses a spouse or any other relative, one usually has the support of family and friends. But I had no one to share my grief with. We didn't have or know any Lesbian friends. We only had each other. I'd had relatives and friends die before, but I'd never shed a tear. But with the death of my Jo, I sobbed my heart out...but only during times I was alone.

During the first year, I visited Joanne's grave every Sunday, bringing her one red rose each time. A family member found out about my secret trips and told me there was no sense in visiting the grave, saying that Jo wasn't there. But the gravesite was the last place I was near her before she was lowered into the ground. Going to the cemetery, sitting by her grave with the red rose, and talking to her made this "our place." I'd tell her how much I missed her, loved her, and that I always would. I was filled with an inner peace on those Sundays, feeling close to her. I sensed Jo could hear me. Ten years since her death, she is still my love. As I heard in *Torch Song Trilogy*, it's hard not to be in love with someone who is dead; they make so few mistakes.

I didn't know how to handle my feelings, so I wrote poetry or messages to her through the years. I sat alone with my sorrow for seven years. The grief wouldn't stop. But in 1987, I finally admitted I was a Lesbian. I hadn't just fallen in love with a woman. I felt scared and didn't know what to do, but I finally was feeling and thinking again.

It was during this time that my mother fell and shattered her shoulder. My mother and I were far from close, but I believed it was my responsibility to take care of her. When her husband died five months later, I gave up my life and moved into her little house. My life felt over again. She wouldn't let me out of her sight, wouldn't let me go anywhere alone. Even though she was in her eighties, I felt she'd outlive me. For more than three years, I saw no way out and contemplated suicide at times.

I wanted to come out to her, but I didn't have the courage to face her disgust of me. I couldn't deal with the humiliation I was certain to feel by her reaction. She is very homophobic. I wanted to tell my grown daughters, but fear of their reaction was more than I could bear. Sometimes I'd think, "I'm 58. Who in the hell would want me anyway?" My loneliness was killing me a little more each day.

I began seeing a therapist, which of course embarrassed my mother. "Why don't you just pull yourself up by your bootstraps and stop being so depressed?" was her attitude. My therapist assured me I wasn't a pervert or abnormal. She told me I can be proud of who I am. I began believing there was a life out there for me and that when I was ready, come hell or high water, I was going to be brave enough to face up to it and begin my life.

I wanted to find happiness for myself. I felt I needed someone to love and someone to love me. My empty feelings made me want to find a support group for shy persons like myself, someday.

Then, on the evening of August 31, 1991, I told my 19 year old granddaughter that I am gay. I told her that if she didn't want anything to do with me or was embarrassed, I would understand. But she rushed over to me and kissed me. "Grams," she said, "I've always loved you. With your trusting me to be the first one you come out to [in the family] I love you even more than ever." I took it all in. "I'm so proud of you, Grams," she continued. "I hope you can find someone and be happy. You deserve it."

I kidded her. "Hey. Do you think you can find a nice lady for your Grams?" We laughed over that and we cried from the intimacy of our sharing, trust and faith.

"I wish I could get Martina [Navratilova] for you, Grams," she said. I had to agree.

I grieved the death of Jo for 10 years. I believe my therapist saved my life. It was through her guidance that I finally admitted to myself that I am a Lesbian. That admission was the first step toward my healing. And so, after several months of therapy, I put my loss behind me and my heart finally healed.

I became braver every day. I started taking risks. I told my mother of my sexuality, which embarrassed her. She "accepts" me, but says she is hurt by this "gay thing."

In January of 1991, I attended my first Lesbian meeting. It was an "over 40" rap group. I went in search of new friends. There were about 10 of us. We stated our names, why we were there, and spoke briefly about our problems and fears. When I heard a certain voice, something stirred inside me. I turned to see the woman speaking and I looked into beautiful blue eyes. My heart skipped a beat.

Like myself, she was a "late bloomer" in the Lesbian world. We became fast friends. Within a week, I was head over heels in love. I adored her, cherished her, and felt our friendship was the kind you only get once or twice in a lifetime. We had much in common, but we did have one major difference. I had made love with a woman. She had not. Had I not been so blinded by my own happiness, good fortune, renewed feelings of self worth, and feeling wanted by this "wonderful" woman, I possibly would have realized that I was about to be used.

When this woman decided we should consummate our union, I was more than ready. We had a wonderful weekend together, and she told me she had "caught a star."

But three days later, I received a box in the mail. It contained video movies and books that I had left at this woman's home. I'd expected that we'd watch movies at her place in the future and that I'd read the books during other times there. Obviously I was wrong.

A letter in the box said she had made a wise choice of partner for her first sexual experience with a woman. She thanked me, but wrote that "it" was over. She wrote that she would never forget me.

The devastation and humiliation I felt were indescribable. I sensed she would hang up if I called, so I wrote a letter telling her I would understand if she did not want me for a life partner and said I understood she used me for her sexual experiment. I believed my love for her could withstand that fact, but I didn't want to lose the friendship. That was too good and important to me. I could survive just being a friend. Three weeks passed. No reply.

I wanted her to answer some questions about myself, so I left a message on her answering machine. I felt desperate. I felt I needed to know what was wrong with me. Why wasn't I wanted or needed as a friend anymore? I asked her to be completely honest and brutal, if necessary. I asked if we could meet and talk over coffee, or even on the phone, if she preferred. If any of this was unacceptable to her, I asked her to call my machine and leave a message telling me to go to hell and that would be that. I promised I would not answer the phone and force her into conversation. She never called.

I cried for two weeks and was suicidal once again. I had previously felt more courage because of the friendship we had had. Because of that, I had told my daughters I am a Lesbian. But with the rejection, I felt made a fool of in front of my family. That was more than I could bear. I even considered going back into the closet. I didn't need that kind of pain.

But thank God for my daughters, a friend of 30 years, and my wonderful therapist. With their support, I began to get back my self-respect. They encouraged me to "get back out there" and I did, going to any group meetings I could find. And I started reading books relating to broken hearts. My therapist suggested *Smart Women, Foolish Choices*. I found that it covers all relationships, courtships and breakups. It addresses how women act and react to adversity, and speaks of foolish mistakes women make in loving.

I think the woman who last stole my heart probably had a good laugh over my naïveté and vulnerability. But she doesn't know what a good education she gave me. I am wiser. I am stronger. I have learned caution. And I have recovered by not letting one despicable, vicious, amoral, narcissistic, manipulative, self-righteous bitch destroy me. I had given this woman the authority to say what was wrong with me. Nothing is wrong with me. I had given to her at my expense, just as I'd done most of my life with many others. I'm learning to recognize my needs and wants and not be a martyr anymore.

I am 59 years old now. A young 59. Sitting around and vegetating is the worst thing anyone can do. So I'm going back to school to become a registered dental assistant. Furthering my education, getting a profession, and getting off Social Security Disability is really boosting my recovery.

I don't want to spend the rest of my life alone. With renewed feelings of self-worth, I am continuing my search for a kind, honest, loving woman with whom I can share my life. I know my soulmate is out there somewhere. Most of all, I know I'm okay and I'm going to make it.

(*Editorial note:* Four months after submitting this story, Lyn sent me a copy of the certificate she received for completing a course toward her goal of a registered dental assistant. "Just wanted you to know that what I stated [about going back to school] was not bullshit." I had no doubt about that, Lyn. No doubt at all.)

Oh, my friend, my love
Is my loneliness
My sadness
Ever going to end?

Hard to believe it's true
No, no you couldn't die
Not you, not ever, God not now.
It's been over 4 months now
That you've been gone
My pain is still there
Still wondering what happened
and how.

Life's not the same without you
Even the sky doesn't seem as blue
Don't smile much anymore
Life now, is really quite a bore.
My friend, my love, I miss you
With all my heart I do.

Doralyn Moran
July, 1980

You turned my life around and for awhile I knew
what it was to be loved, to be needed. Then time
ran out, destiny stepped in and interceded.

My world stopped that day. There's just no life
without you, I'm so lost there's nothing but pain.

Blue skies, sunshine, gentle rain, they have no
meaning anymore. I can't feel anything, except the pain.

It took most of my life to find you, things were
so right, the future so bright, and in the blink
of an eye it was all taken away. Now I'm alone
again and all I can do is cry. I cry for you and
for me, I cry for all that was to be.

I'll never be the same again. A special time in
my life has come to an end.

I'll grow old and gray, you'll not age a day.
I'll grow old with sorrow, we missed all of tomorrow.

The saddest thing for me to do
Is to grow old without you.

Doralyn Moran
October 22, 1980

If only it were possible to see you
For an hour, even for a minute
Just one more time.

I often wonder if you'll be there
Waiting for me at my time.

If of that I could be sure
I think maybe I could endure.

It's a year since the day my life was shattered.
A year of emotions being tattered.
A year of my heart being broken
and for the words never spoken.

A year of crying and grief.
A year of anger and frustration.
A year of loneliness.
A year of sadness beyond belief.

My head says it's time now for healing.
But my heart can't lose that empty feeling.
I know in time I'll mend
But till my life comes to an end
I'll always miss you my friend.

Doralyn Moran
March 19, 1981

It's Christmas time already
My first Christmas without you
It's not gonna be easy
It's not gonna be the same.

Just thinking of you
makes my hands unsteady
The holidays were always so special
Oh how you loved them, your time of year
I'll try to carry on for you
But not this year.

This year's too soon, the pain too great
This year's for memories, all of them so dear.
Memories are all I have left of you.
My memories will have to see me through
Remembering your smiling face, the touch
of your hand, your pure joy of giving.
Such joy at just living.

Christmas doesn't mean so much this year,
My first Christmas without you.

Doralyn Moran
1980

1984

My dear...my very missed lover and partner
J'm healing
But J miss you so.
Don't think J will ever stop.

You were a part of my life
You always will be.

J miss you babe.

Doralyn Moran

1990

God, J can't believe it, ten years since you left me and life.
The more J read, the more J search for answers, the more
J wonder what the hell it's all about.

J've learned without love to give and receive, life is
meaningless and worthless.
These past ten years have been an eternity.
J haven't gone on with my life and after all these years
there are feelings and emotions emerging...
and J don't quite know how to handle them, kiddo.

Haven't had the courage to come out publicly and this
all of a sudden is tearing me apart.
Wish J could tell my kids who and what J am so that
they would know me and J could look for love again.

You and J know it's time for me to move on with my life.
Wish J had your courage Jo...J've never had it.
J admired you so much for that.
You know, J don't have to tell you...J will always love you...
You will always be in my heart.

We are soul mates...we will meet again.
Until then....

Me

Doralyn Moran

My lover and I had many mutual friends. But since she's died, I'm invited out less and less. This is only worsening my loneliness. I feel like the "odd woman out" in addition to having to deal with the loss of my partner. What can I do?

It's sad, but true. Many times when our relationships change, whether by death or breakup, so do our friendships. Having someone we love die is very difficult whether the death be sudden or from a lengthy disease. The loneliness you're experiencing is expected and this feeling could be exacerbated because you're with couples, you and your spouse's friends, who you mutually shared social time with. More than ever, you need to be around people you can commiserate with about your loss. Perhaps there are one or two in your couple group you can share your feelings with. This is not to put them on the spot, but only to express your own feelings of loss and loneliness. You definitely need to seek out new friends you share interests with. This is important. Get involved with clubs or do volunteer work in the community. In time you'll feel like dating. This is not advisable until you have grieved your loss and feel more resolved in your heart that life for you has to go on.

WENDY

Clutching to your tee shirt
I smell your scent
and my eyes well with unrelenting sadness and tears.

Grief is cruel and lonely.
I've screamed in the car,
cried down the pain,
but it doesn't cease.

You're gone from me and I do the best that I can.

Sometimes I'm okay.
Other times I'm miserable.
Your death was so sudden,
so unexpected.
I'm left
alone
single again, feeling like an unacknowledged widow.

I made a collage out of your pictures.
You were so cute in your childhood pictures,
especially the one of you sitting with Santa.
You looked so innocent.

Even with such an unbearable childhood,
your strength and inner courage brought you seven
years of light
out of the darkness.

You were turning the corner.
You were loved, Wendy,
and I can't imagine my life can go on without you,
yet, it has.
It has because of your love for me.
I know you'd want me to go on,
and that someday we will be together again.

Linda St. Pierre

Invisible Widow
by Linda St. Pierre

I've never appreciated people who've said to me, "No pain, no gain," or being told I should be grateful for a "growth experience" after going through a terribly difficult event in my life.

In 1982, I suffered the loss of my best friend Maureen. The aneurysm gave no warning.

In 1987, my father died of a massive heart attack in a blizzard. The police had to drive me to the hospital because the main roads were closed.

But neither experience prepared me for the sudden death of my partner, Wendy, on November 17, 1989. Wendy was 38 years old, working as a substance abuse counselor at Rutgers University at the time of her death. She was in the process of completing her certification for that occupation. As a recovering person herself, she enjoyed sharing her strength and hope with others. She was a dedicated member of Alcoholics Anonymous and considered AA her family.

The last time I saw Wendy was at her favorite place, Donaldson Park. Since giving up cigarettes, she had started walking two miles a day. I stopped by the park on a whim, as it wasn't my usual day to be out of the office.

Wendy looked very pale and didn't feel well. She had just gotten her period and complained of menstrual cramps. That wasn't unusual. We talked and then I got back into my car. As she walked away, I beeped my horn. She turned to me and waved good-bye.

Wendy was on her way to work after an AA meeting when she hit a medium-sized truck. She kept driving. She was also speeding. The truck driver said she was stopped at a traffic light when he caught up to her. He told her she'd hit his truck, but she hadn't realized she had. Her last words before passing out were, "I'm dying, and I want to go home."

A police officer came to our apartment that night and told me that Wendy was unconscious in the emergency room of the hospital. He suggested family members be called immediately. After having experienced my best friend's and Dad's sudden deaths, it ran through my mind that Wendy had already died.

Unable to drive, I called Wendy's brother. Just as when my father had died, I stood outside the apartment waiting for a ride to the hospital.

After three hours of neurosurgery, we were told there was extensive brain damage, but the doctors didn't know why. A brain tumor or aneurysm was suspected. Blood flooded Wendy's brain cavity and she was given a 20% chance of survival. A respirator kept her alive.

I don't know how I would have survived those days without my belief in God and the compassionate, loving friends of ours. An AA friend stayed with me during the surgery and others joined me in the morning. Unfortunately, Wendy's family was very inconsistent with her. They'd withdraw their concern for her periodically, causing her much turmoil. With this in mind, I had my mother stay at our apartment while I was gone, in case Wendy's family would try to enter. Even our minister advised me to change the door locks because he wasn't sure what Wendy's family was capable of.

Wendy's mother called me the morning of her death. She wanted to know where Wendy's jewelry was. I didn't understand this concern at a time like that and feared her family would come with a moving van and attempt to dismantle our apartment. Fortunately, this fear didn't materialize.

I drifted through the funeral, in shock and denial. Wendy and I had been together three years. We had just completed one year of living together and were very dedicated to one another. We'd worked our separate "programs" and were willing to face problems within our relationship. Ours wasn't a "perfect" relationship, but our home life was an important focus for us.

Initially, I did everything I thought was "right." I sat with Wendy's family at the funeral. I even read the prayer of St. Francis at the service. I used the tools I'd learned from my Overeaters Anonymous Program and attended meetings. Slogans such as "This too shall pass" were friends through the most painful times.

But six months later, the shock wore off, the calls came less frequently, the support network decreased and I began to isolate. I learned what "quiet desperation" means. The pain and loss overwhelmed me, even though I'd had good support before. I got mad at God and stopped going to church. I read all the books on grief and hated them all.

I couldn't understand why this had happened to me. What did I do to deserve this? There were no answers. Depression took over, as well as a sense of hopelessness. One night I thought of suicide and how I hoped to be killed in a car accident so I wouldn't have to feel the terrible loss and pain.

But I became frightened when I thought of suicide a second time. I told someone close to me about my feelings and how I didn't think I could go on living without my Wendy.

I was in therapy where I did a lot of crying. But my therapist's office didn't have a monopoly on my tears. I cried and screamed in my car. I cried at the shopping center where we used to shop together. I cried as I sat in our apartment's parking space, knowing "our" apartment was devoid of Wendy's spirit and enthusiasm.

When the intense feelings appeared (sometimes frequently), I held onto my program slogans. Some nights I called people that loved and cared about me. Sometimes I went to bed early or read some writings about hope.

In looking for supportive resources, I found that the grief group at a local hospital didn't fit my needs. It was difficult for me to talk to the group about my experiences and I got frustrated. So I am considering starting a Widow's Group in New Jersey. I've been in touch with three other widows and hope we can find strength and respect for each other in a group setting.

I've had a difficult time letting go of Wendy's clothing. It's been almost a year since she died and I can't bring myself to discard them. It's so hard. My advice to anyone else in this situation is to know there are no set limits...when you are ready to let go, you will. I have faith that this will happen for me.

I have a lot of gratitude today and I have a healthy respect for the slogan "One day at a time." That is how I live my life today.

As for my loss...I shared love and life with a very special person. No one can take that away.

One Each

Papa always had sense.
He never criticized my husband, nor my taste in men.

Mother's husband took us both in his arms...
one each.

He loved to sit with us outside on warm evenings
and watch as thunderstorms built, boomed and then
passed.

He took me out to dinner on the day my divorce was final.
Then he drove to the cemetery to tell Mom.

Papa smiled softly when J told him J was a Lesbian...
and again when J said J was in love.

He had such wonderful insight, J think he already knew.
Why didn't he tell me?

He dressed up for my wedding. His gift to us was a tatted
table setting Mother had made when they were young.

Father sat with me in the hospital after the accident...
and again at the funeral parlour.

Papa helped me cry when J was exhausted and dry.

He had loved us both and took us in his arms...
one each.

Carol Wood

Epilog—
One Last Thought

Love after Love
after Love after
and Finally

you arrive in the arms
of your favorite chair
and drink the tea
that has been left
just for you.
At the bottom of the cup

you find the stranger
who knows you bone by bone
who has been waiting patiently
all this time
for you to discover the only one
who will always love you.

Smile at your own reflection.
Gather yourself up
and be your own child
sitting on your own lap.
Rest your cheek on your own bent knee.
Forgive yourself.   Live.

Lesléa Newman

Contributors' Notes

Jean M. Allen is presently an independent contractor for two different firms and lives with her cat in her comfortable house in Ferndale, Michigan. Her background is varied: military, police officer, nuclear power plant security, social worker, and volunteer domestic violence worker. "I hope my input to this book is helpful to others...which is the goal in my life."

Patti Azevedo, a native Californian, is living in the moment, discovering each and every one in her cast of many characters, and finally enjoying life as a recently described Lesbian. "This is my first actual publication and I'm happy to say my relationship in the poem survived! My love for my partner continues to change, grow, thrive, and deepen each day."

Michelle Bancroft: "I'm a 26 year old dyke who is proof that you can experience loss in your life, survive it, and even prosper from it. I'm a full-time student and writer now living in beautiful northern California. My hope is that sharing my personal experiences, as I have here, will send the message of healing and hope to all women in need."

Ryma Birch embarked on an extensive inner survey of soul making, following travel on four continents. She finished a Ph.D. program at the same time she attended a dying friend who brought her "into the light." Learning to heal onto death and life was a gift: She embraced herself as a wounded healer. Ryma's work in life is to facilitate creativity, health, and empowerment in women and children. Writing for her is a prophetic act as she continues to come out.

Cathy Chambers is "busy trying to keep a life while in school for a Masters in Library Science."

Charlie: "I am now 30 years old. I feel I've changed a great deal, some for the best, some not. I don't ever plan on pursuing my modeling, due to many physical disabilities. I always had a simple dream, though, and it has come true. I now have a small house, my pets, and a car. I keep myself busy most of the time by working in my yard or on my house. I'm also going to school taking basics, retraining my brain. Plus I work out with weights one hour every other day to keep up my strength. I've begun dating again, no one serious, though. It will be a long while for that, if ever. I've been meeting new people, doing new things. I still get very depressed at times, sometimes to the point of wanting to die, but I get myself out of that real quick. I used to say, life sucks, but now I say life is okay. Hopefully someday I'll be able to say, life is great!"

Claire Connelly is volunteer Executive Director of Gay and Lesbian Resources of Ventura County, California, where she counsels clients and performs ministerial services, among other duties. Claire is working toward licensure as a family counselor and recently completed her master's thesis on *Homosexual Psyche: Development and Psychosocial Issues*. She is in her mid-fifties and has a 24-year-old son through a prior marriage. Claire worked in publishing as an editor, writer, and graphic artist in New York, Connecticut, and California. She gives workshops on gay/lesbian issues throughout southern California and is a Red Cross certified HIV/AIDS educator. Claire is a founding member of NOW. She is an active member of Metropolitan Community Church Ventura and of Southern California Women for Understanding. She has come under fire from lesbians who advocate sex without love or commitment. "I believe an interchange of sexual energy without love or outside the context of a committed relationship is unhealthy physically and emotionally, although I respect everyone's right to choose their own values."

Rachel D. is a pseudonym for a scientist who lives in Los Angeles with two cats. She is choosing to be anonymous due to the traditions of AA and Al-Anon. Her fantasy is to own a big old house, support herself as a fiction writer, and hire someone else to mow the lawn.

Isabel DeMaris is a musician, artisan, athlete, business professional learning to live and love happily in central Massachusetts. A 1984 graduate of Boston University, she performs regularly with several community orchestras, works on her song writing, turns bowls from wood, sweats it out on the soccer and softball fields and manages a Book Distribution Center for a major publisher. She is learning, very slowly, to accept the love of family and friends.

Diane De Moon currently lives in L.A. with her cat. They are very happy together. She says, "I enjoy writing in general and also enjoy composing music. I really don't know what to think about relationships anymore. None of them seem to be long-lasting. Most of them look scary. Maybe someday I'll make another attempt, but I don't count on it. I've learned to be happy with myself and I'm very independent. I do some dating. I find that most women want to suffocate me to death. Let me breathe, please! Why should I subject myself to these characters? So I don't. I haven't given up–I'm just not impressed with a lot of the things that go on."

Sara Edelstein: "I'm originally from the Midwest, but I've lived in Portland, Oregon for almost 20 years. Along with many other baby boomers, I took a good many years working at odd jobs and generally deciding what I was doing in life. Currently, I write fiction and nonfiction, teach at a local college, and garden enthusiastically. Having recovered from the breakup in my story, I live with my partner and our dog and cat. Sara Edelstein is the writing name I use to separate my writing life, teacher life, and personal life."

Ginny Foster continues to live alone and write in Portland, Oregon. She does features and profiles for the Northwest Examiner newspaper and piece-meal editing jobs. Having won a week at a writers' retreat house in Rockaway Beach, she finished the final draft of a play. This year she is also a member of the Frequent Traveler Panel for Greyhound Bus, and answers survey questions about restrooms, etc. throughout the Northwest.

Ruby J.C. Fowler is a learning-disabled Southern gal born in Atlanta, Georgia in 1949 of working-class parents. As a teenager, she would sit up until the early hours of the morning, jazzed on instant coffee and Creamora, hamming out tormented poetry, and has continued writing ever since (give or take some cumulative years of Writer's Block). She left the South when she was 18 and moved to Springfield, Massachusetts, where she remained until 1980. At age 30, she moved to San Francisco and has lived there ever since. Ruby is currently working on an anthology of short stories about butch/femme lifestyles and generic gender-fuck. She is also a member of the Mothertongue Readers Theater Collective. She is in substance abuse and codependency recovery and is very happy to be alive, although frantically searching for her inner kids. If you happen to run into them, please send them home.

Susan J. Friedman: "I am a 31 year old Jewish lesbian living in the Boston area. In thinking back on these poems (I wrote them well over a year ago), I feel like it is important to say how much healing has come into my life since then. Endings, painful as they are, are also beginnings. This beginning, for me, has meant learning how to live alone for the first time, and feeling what a blessing friends are in my life. It has also been a period of re-birth for my writing. So, I guess my message to other hurting folks is to hang in there–it gets better!"

Kaye Hunter: "I'm proud to be a native Texan, reared in a small west Texas town. I now live just north of Dallas with my lover and her three wonderful children and am quite happy. I teach elementary school and am actively involved in the education field. I'm working toward my Master of Science degree at Texas Women's University in Denton, Texas. Writing has been a lifelong hobby, and there have been many moments in my life that I would not have been able to endure without my journal and a pen."

Tighe Instone: "Pakeha–born 1940, Aotearoa/New Zealand. After 48 years of city living is now rejuvenating in a rural valley. Diverse experience in the paid work force includes factories, newspaper, cabaret, public service, general and psychiatric nursing, abortion clinic. Present work is with a feminist health collective, *The Health Alternatives for Women*. Over 20 years progressed from organizing lesbian parties and dances to organizing rallies and marches. Special interests: Lesbian politics, ethics and visibility, and self determination for the Tangata Whenua of Aotearoa (indigenous people of Aotearoa). Always a teller of tales–now trying to make time to write them down."

Janet Lawson: "I was born in Hamilton, Ontario. My passion is the ocean and I intend to sail around the world someday. I believe I am both a writer and an artist. I consider the practice of law to be my 'day job.' I have been clean and sober 16 years. I'm 38 now. At the moment, I am committed to therapy so I don't keep making the same mistakes over and over. I love life, even though sometimes it's the pits."

Elaine Leeder is a therapist and educator. When not healing from breakup, she writes about radical women's history and violence in relationships, in addition to biking, swimming, and traveling. In everything she does, she attempts to do it "write from the heart."

Susan McConnell-Celi was a member of the New York chapter of Daughters of Bilitis from 1966 through 1970. In 1970, she was active in NOW, founder of the Alliance of Women for Equality, and co-founder of the first Gay Activist Alliance Chapter in New Jersey. In 1971, she was co-founder of the New Jersey Lesbian Mother's Union. McConnell-Celi holds a Bachelor's degree in education from Seton Hall University and a Master's degree from Kean College. She has taught English since 1970, as well as teaching college in the 80's. She is the first lesbian educator as a commissioner on the Monmouth County Human Relations Commission. McConnell-Celi co-hosted *On the Line*, a weekly radio show now airing as *Lesbian Voices*. She is the mother of four children and the proud grandparent of three.

Doralyn Moran was born September 20, 1931. She's a native Californian, was married 17 years, has "three beautiful, married daughters, nine grandchildren, and a great grandchild on the way." She was a dental assistant many years, then medical assistant and medical office manager. Illness forced her onto Social Security Disability in 1988. In July, 1991, she returned to school, earning a certificate in Dental Radiology. She's working toward her State Boards for Registered Dental Assistant in late 1992. "I dedicate my story to Chris Garcia, therapist, friend extraordinaire. She knew just the right time to push and put the proverbial boot in the proper place. I owe you my life."

Ruth Mountaingrove: "I am close to 69 than 68. Since leaving my 13 year partner, I have earned an MA in Art (for) Photography, moved to another state, have frequent exhibitions of my paintings, and a photography process I call Drawing with Light. I have continued writing poetry, non-fiction, and short story. I have also continued to sing and write songs. I have a lover two years older than I am. My oldest relationship (25 years) is with my Mustang convertible."

Lesléa Newman is the author of a dozen books including *Sweet Dark Places, A Letter to Harvey Milk, Secrets,* and *Heather Has Two Mommies.* Her newest novel, *In Every Laugh a Tear,* will be published in the fall of 1992.

Cris Newport was awarded a B.A. in English and Creative Writing from the University of Massachusetts at Boston after returning to school in her late twenties. A year later, she received a Masters in Teaching from Tufts University. In her spare time, she reviews books for *Bay Windows, off our backs,* and a Boston-based radio program called *Brand New Day.* Her fiction has appeared in *Common Lives/Lesbian Lives, Test Tube Women,* and *Lesbian Bedtime Stories II.* Her novel *Sparks Might Fly* will be published by New Victoria Publishers in 1993. She is currently an Assistant Professor of English at a two-year college in New Hampshire.

Anita L. Pace is amazed she's actually publishing this book! She has a B.A. in Social Welfare, has written a screenplay that she handed to Carol Burnett (but never sold) and has had several stories printed in newspapers. She has also contributed to two other anthologies. She recently escaped Los Angeles for the Portland, Oregon area, which she hopes will never become L.A. Northwest. Her goals include writing several more books, helping get a good Democrat in the White House soon, getting over her fear of flying and computers, seeing Hawaii and Europe, having a satisfying relationship that lasts the rest of her life, and overcoming her fear of death before dying. She also believes Anita Hill.

Karla Pettit wants to drive a Harley across the United States, although she fears she might be shot by Bubba in the South. "Actually, I would like to own my own business, possibly a woman's full service salon."

Lupe Anne Reuben: "I am interested in animal rights and the environment. If I knew then what I know now, I would have studied piano instead of playing so much baseball. Creating things, whether stories, music, furniture, or whatever, gives my life meaning, as does a healthy relationship with a life partner."

Romeo lives in Portland. I'm a hopeless romantic, but I'm having to learn how to trust again as well as who to trust."

Jodi Silverman graduated with honors with a B.S. degree in Psychology from Brooklyn College in Brooklyn, New York. She then went on the get her Masters in Social Work from Adelphi University in New York. In 1988, Jodi moved to Connecticut with her present lover of 4 years. In Connecticut, Jodi received her C.I.S.W. certification. She has a private practice catering to lesbians in Branford, Connecticut and works full time as a Social Worker for the State. This is her first public writing.

Marie Skonieczny is originally from Chicago. She is an accountant and has recently established a music publishing and production company. She began writing songs in 1974, although she didn't pursue a career in music until 1989 after she moved to L.A. She now works two careers, but hopes to eventually have only music as her career. "However," she says, "accounting knowledge and experience is not a bad asset to have when starting a business." Her works usually make a statement of current societal trends and are usually not commercial, although she does write commercially if it has the potential to make a positive contribution to society. Some of her songs have a 60's style to them. She believes that there is not enough being said or done by individuals of this generation as compared to the 60s. "We need to get radical again," says Marie.

Linda St. Pierre: "I have been a Social Worker for almost twenty years. I work with low income families. I have an ACSW and enjoy working with groups. I wrote my story while attending a retreat in a small town at the Jersey shore called Harvey Cedars, on Long Beach Island. It's a very peaceful and spiritual space for me. My motivation for writing was to help other lesbians whose hearts have been broken. It's a difficult process, but you find the inner strength and courage to go on."

Jessica Fair Stevens: "Brooklyn-New York City-Portland. twenty-nine year old writer/artist in search (to date) the writer: manque"

Randy Turoff is a freelance writer. She has published numerous poems, stories, and articles. She is the former founding editor of *Womentide*, Provincetown's Lesbian magazine. Currently, Randy works on the staff of *The San Francisco Bay Times*. She was the 1990 GPLA (Gay and

Lesbian Press Association) recipient of the Wallace Hamilton Award for cultural reporting.

Anne Wolf-Grey is an artist and interpretive naturalist living in the Portland, Oregon area. She is enjoying her life.

Carol Wood, born into a military family and later entering the military herself, has been a nomad of sorts for all of her 35 years. Of late, she has returned to the Pacific Northwest for the beauty of both the geography and the people. Being a parent, artist and writer take up most of her time, but there are the occasional mini-vacations to Seattle, the Olympic Peninsula, and Victoria, B.C. Her writing is atypical of most lesbian/feminist work in that it is sprinkled with supportive male characters, and focuses more on being human than on being either homo/heterosexual. She is not only a poet, but has written much in the way of short fiction and erotica, all of which peel away layer after layer of her interesting life revealing an ongoing Spiritual Quest.

zana: "writing this article was part of a very long process of recovery from that particular relationship, and reassessment of my relationship patterns in general. i spent five years celibate. in my current relationship, i'm delighted to find the work paying off in really significant ways! i'm 44, jewish, disabled, working with sister homelands on earth to establish land trust communities for wimin. i can be reached c/o SHE, p.o. box 5285, tucson, arizona 85703."

About the Editor

Anita Louise Pace grew up in Inglewood, California in an American-Italian household. She lived in the Los Angeles area until 1991 when she moved to Oregon. She has a Bachelor's Degree in Social Welfare and studied screenwriting at the Hollywood Scriptwriting Institute. Ms. Pace became severely disabled from Panic Disorder and Agoraphobia in 1978, which prompted her to begin writing. She's authored two stories in other anthologies: "Living With a Hidden Disability–Agoraphobia" (*With the Power of Each Breath*, Cleis Press) and "And Baby Makes Two" (*Cats and Their Dykes*, HerBooks). (Baby was euthanized in February, 1992 at the age of 18.) Ms. Pace lives with her partner, Harriet, with their Holland Lop, Espresso, and a rambunctious Siberian puppy named Matika. She is working on her next book about her childhood family.

About the Therapist

Dakota Sands, MSW, is a licensed psychotherapist with more than 10 years experience in the field. She conducts groups on how to live through a break-up and overcome a broken heart. She also specializes in working with multi-cultural, multi-racial individuals, and with adults abused as children. Ms. Sands is a referred therapist for the *Gay and Lesbian Community Services Center* in Los Angeles, California, where she has a private practice.

She wanted to participate in this anthology as part of her own recovery from a relationship loss. She sees value in lesbians writing their stories and poems for their own personal growth, as well as for the value that shared experiences have for us all. The message we hear, she believes, is that we are not alone in what we are feeling. In that, there is some comfort and knowledge that we can get through the pain of a lost relationship. Furthermore, our lives can open up to more opportunities and a stronger sense of self than we had known before.

♥ To obtain more copies of *Write from the Heart...Lesbians Healing from Heartache,* send $10.95 for each copy to Baby Steps Press, P.O. Box 1917, Beaverton, Oregon 97075. Please include $3.50 shipping and handling per order for up to four books, $5.00 per order for 4-20 books. For larger orders, please write to Baby Steps Press to make arrangements.